MC MEANS

MOVE THE CLASS

*How to Spark Engagement and Motivation in
Urban and Culturally Diverse Classrooms*

DR. SHAUN WOODLY

MC Means Move the Class: How to Spark Engagement and
Motivation in Urban and Culturally Diverse Classrooms
© 2018 by Shaun Woodly, Ph.D.
www.ShaunWoodly.com

Published by Ideal Education Consulting, LLC, Atlanta, GA

Library of Congress Control Number: 2018912390
Paperback ISBN: 978-1-7328481-1-5
Ebook ISBN: 978-1-7328481-0-8

To the educators who lead and teach the children of our future, this book is dedicated to you.

TRACK LIST

INTRODUCTION

AN EDUCATIONAL GROOVE SLIGHTLY TRANSFORMED

Here it is, an educational groove that is slightly transformed. Just a bit of a break from the norm of books you read about teaching. These opening sentences pay homage to one of my all-time favorite hip-hop songs: DJ Jazzy Jeff and the Fresh Prince's "Summertime." It's the quintessential definition of a classic. It's one of those songs that makes you feel good, and for me the summer doesn't really begin until I've heard that song played at a ridiculous volume. That's just me. However, what some do not realize is the music from song is actually sampled. It is a bit of an updated (at the time), enhanced, and re-imagined version of Kool and the Gang's "Summer Madness."

DJ Jazzy Jeff and the Fresh Prince took the foundation of "Summer Madness" and added their own personal spin and creativity to take it from an instrumental, relaxing and smooth track to one of those songs that almost makes you smell BBQ when you hear it.

It's that kind of sampling that I've done with the ideas in this book. I've taken some of the research and proven methods that I and countless other educators have used to be successful in urban and culturally diverse classrooms and added my own personal spin and creativity. I do not want this to be a textbook with complicated jargon and fluff, nor do I want it to be something that won't give value to you. I want this to be a book you can enjoy reading and learn from at the same time.

My goal is to introduce you to the elements of urban education and some ideas that can fundamentally change your classroom in ways that will make teaching more enjoyable and meaningful, and, most importantly, promote higher student achievement. Make no mistake, I am not saying these elements of urban education will solve all teaching problems forevermore. What I am saying is that an understanding of these concepts lays a strong foundation for how you can better connect with *all* of your students and respond better to difficult circumstances in ways that won't have you wanting to jump into your car and curse at the end of each school day.

During the golden age of hip-hop, the rap duo Eric B. & Rakim set speakers everywhere on fire with one of the most iconic rap songs of the '80s, "Eric B. is President." The opening lines are: "I came in the door, I said it before, I never let the mic magnetize me no more..."[1] Known as one of, if not *the*, most influential DJ/MC collaborations in all of hip-hop, Eric B. & Rakim represent the place I was raised and hold near and dear to my heart: Long Island, New York. But a deeper connection with these two takes place for me in the second verse of that song. Rakim is on the mic, staking his claim that it's time to build and for Eric as the DJ to be easy on the cut (scratching & mixing), no mistakes allowed, because to him, his role as the MC was not just a title—MC means move the crowd.

 ## AS A TEACHER, MY ROLE IS ALSO TO BE THE SOURCE OF MOTIVATION, ENERGY, AND HYPE FOR MY STUDENTS.

That line, "MC means move the crowd," always stuck out to me because there was so much to it below the surface. To inspire and motivate an entire group of people is not an easy feat. It became clear to me that moving the crowd meant being the source of motivation, energy, and hype. That is why to Rakim MC is not just a title, but a responsibility.

As a teacher, my role is also to be the source of motivation, energy, and hype for my students, but as it relates to learning. It is not just a title, but a responsibility. That is why, to me, MC means Move the Class.

Because the challenges educators face are great, I'll provide you with some easy-to-digest, but research-based, ideas to help you Move the Class. This book offers you simple stories and lessons learned in 12+ years as an educator in urban or culturally diverse schools, years that were also spent as a DJ. You see, almost every weekend, after a week of teaching and instruction, I would pack up my turntables, mixer, and microphone and take my talents to a variety of venues or events and move the crowd. My job there was simple in theory, but extremely difficult to execute well, just like teaching.

While Eric B. & Rakim had the benefit of one another as they set the stage on fire as a next-level DJ/MC duo, I on the other hand was a one-man show on the weekends. I was both the DJ and I was also the MC. Now I imagine you might be asking what in the world teaching *really* has to do with two turntables and a mic?[2] I'm glad you asked. Let me tell you a story about what can happen when you're able to Move the Class, then break down these elements, one by one, in each of the following chapters/tracks. Allow me to introduce one of my former students, Jonathan.

One day I had one of those cherished opportunities to enjoy a moment of semi-serenity and quiet, that valued time when your room is empty because students are at lunch and you have a moment to catch your breath. But, like most teachers, I didn't have time for that. There are copies to be made (if the copy machine is working) and learning experiences to be planned. So with that, I used this time to head to the teachers' lounge and make some copies of a handout for my students to take home. This brief trip of serenity, however, would be quickly derailed by a student who decided to make some poor decisions during his class.

Walking down the hall, copy paper in hand, I saw just ahead Ms. Green stumble in frustration out into the hallway. She looked at me and didn't have to say a word—the expression on her face read *Help me...please!*

"Mr. Woodly, can you please talk to him? He won't listen to me," she said to me as she explained her difficulty of trying to get a student to follow some relatively simple instructions during class. I had been looking forward to the opportunity to make my copies in peace, and maybe even treat myself to a frosty beverage if time allowed. But from the look of despair on her face, I knew this teacher needed some backup and I had no problem delaying my plans to help her out. I quickly peeked into the classroom to see a particular student joyfully entertaining his classmates, seemingly celebrating how he successfully flustered his teacher. Quickly stepping back into the hallway, Ms. Green, with a look of frustration, briefly explained how her student, Jonathan, refused to sit down, made all sorts of inappropriate noises in the middle of class, and was an all-around disruption.

Ms. Green was a promising first-year teacher who wanted to enjoy teaching and was dedicated to her craft and her students, but she clearly struggled. She explained that Jonathan started the day off OK, but wouldn't participate in the class activities and gave minimal effort, if any, on his assignments and tasks. It eventually escalated to the point where he began to find ways to entertain himself—during instructional time. She went on to tell me how over the course of the day she tried to calmly talk to him several times and gave him a warning that he'd be written up with an administrative referral if he did not change his behavior. Ms. Green told me that he might stop for a moment or two, but soon he would inevitably pick up right where he left off. From the way she explained it, I could tell there was more to the story about Jonathan's behavior and, had time allowed, she could have provided me more detail. Since we were, for this brief moment, standing in the hallway, we knew it was important that instruction resume soon. So she asked again, "Can you please talk him? I don't know what else to do."

"Sure," I said. "I'd be glad to."

Jonathan had given Ms. Green a year's worth of stress in a day's time. He was a student I was familiar with, as I taught him the year before. He was one of those students you know is smart, but gives little, if any, effort when he doesn't find value in what is being learned. But he likes attention and uses his intellect to consistently step right up to, and sometimes even cross, the proverbial line of frustration for his teachers. That's how he chooses to engage while in school.

I made my way to Ms. Green's doorway and stood there, waiting for him to see me. Not two seconds later, he turned to see me there staring right at him. I made direct eye contact, not saying a word, and he froze. I made a simple gesture, my index finger signaling him to "come here," but my eyes saying "bring your lil' so-and-so here, now!" Jonathan complied with no hesitation. As he made his way to the hallway, his entire demeanor changed. I took him for a brief walk with me to make the copies and we began to have a conversation about how he needed to check his behavior—real quick. This allowed Ms. Green to redirect the rest of the class and resume instruction.

Ms. Green had gotten to the point where she felt like she was at school every day with a goal to just make it to 3 o'clock. Do enough so that some semblance of learning is occurring and no one gets hurt, then she can go home. Just make it to 3 o'clock - the end of the day. I meet a lot of teachers whose mission each day is to make it to whatever time they can look up to feel the relief that they're able to send students on their way. For many, this profession is not what they thought it would be. They're not impacting the lives of students in the ways they thought possible. And beyond all of this, every day seems to get progressively more difficult.

I returned moments later to bring Jonathan back to class so that he wouldn't miss anything else. I waited for him to deliver the apology we discussed and went on with my day. Whether you've been in the classroom 10 days or 10 years, it's not hard to tell that some students react differently to some educators over others, but why? No classroom or teacher is perfect. However, it can appear that some have a much easier time than others. In some classrooms, everything seems to flow, students are engaged with the learning, and there are little to no behavioral issues. You know that class, right? Yes, that one.

What I was able to do with Jonathan was very intentional— it was very relational. This is because when Jonathan was a student in my classroom I was able to provide an environment that allowed him to be great in his own way. As a result, Jonathan, among the other students, chose to not only cooperate, but let his genius absolutely shine in my class. This level of understanding and respect for me proved to benefit him academically while he was in my class and beyond, which is why I was able to easily connect with him even after he was no longer a student of mine.

As you make your way through this book, you'll learn about the specifics as to why I was able to quickly resolve that issue for Ms. Green. You'll also learn how, with some adjustments, you too can create the type of learning environment where the learning is so engaging, the motivation is so high, and the relationships so genuine that there isn't even time for students to misbehave. It can be done.

AS EDUCATORS, WE HAVE THE SINGLE MOST IMPORTANT PROFESSION ON THE FACE OF THIS EARTH—AND THAT IS NOT UP FOR DEBATE.

#MOVETHECLASS

If you teach in an urban or multicultural school setting, it's likely you know a student like Jonathan. You likely also know a myriad of different types of students, from different types of backgrounds, all with different types of untapped potential. But you also likely know students for whom life outside of those school walls is not easy. We have students dealing with issues that range from poverty, to neglect, and even drug exposure. Lack of parental involvement leaves some of our students with more responsibilities than any child should ever have. We have a significant number of students who come from homes where English is not the first language, which creates a language barrier. Now, for a moment, put yourself in that child's shoes.

Imagine what it's like for a student to come to your class, a place that may be their only safe haven, only to walk in the doors and feel like they do not belong or are not wanted. We have students who are steadily losing hope in education because they do not connect with, or see little to no purpose in, what is being learned. Imagine the implications for that student to come into your class only for this cycle of no educational value or purpose to continue, eventually leading to yet another dropout. There are so many challenges that both students and educators face, but I am here to tell you that all is not lost. By no means!

MC Means Move the Class is for you if:

- you teach culturally diverse students and can't seem to break through the barriers to make connections.

- you want to enjoy teaching more, but find that there's no excitement in your room, for the students or you.

- you teach students with difficult home lives and are having a tough time getting through to them.

- no matter what you do, you cannot seem to tap into your students' motivation, and apathy has taken a permanent seat in your room.

- you want to empower staff members or colleagues with the strategies necessary to be successful with their students.

As educators, we have the single most important profession on the face of this earth—and that is not up for debate. Literally no other careers or opportunities would exist without teachers. We are that important. In our multicultural and urban schools, we have to be good at what we do. As a matter of fact, we have to be *great* at what we do for the sake of the unforeseen future. That's a lot easier said than done, I know. So, how do we do this? How do we transform teaching and learning in our classrooms and schools?

We Move the Class, that's how.

End Notes

1. "Eric B. is President" (Eric B. & Rakim, 1986) Zakia Records

2. "Two Turntables and a Mic" (Black Moon, 1999) Priority Records, Duck Down

3. "Summer Madness" (Kool and the Gang), 1974. De-Lite Records

    The introduction's title is a play on the lyrics from "Summertime" (DJ Jazzy Jeff & the Fresh Prince, 1991). Jive Records

SIDE A

TRACK 1

YOU CAN CULTURALLY GET WITH THIS, OR YOU CAN CULTURALLY GET WITH THAT

*Creating a learning environment that
helps students of color thrive*

Even without stepping foot in your classroom, it is highly likely I can tell you exactly what's going to happen there. Research shows that we have reached the point where we can predict the academic success of a student based solely on that child's status as a cultural minority. Many well-intentioned teachers suffer from high levels of stress and low levels of motivation as they struggle to help their African American, Asian American, Latinx, Native American, and low-income students reach their fullest potential, never finding the solution to truly helping their students or themselves.

Reflecting the ideas of an iconic hip-hop song, *you can get with this*[1]: Create a learning environment that helps culturally diverse students thrive, increasing your effectiveness and decreasing your stress.

Or you can get with that[1]: Continue to "get by," not enjoying what you do day to day, and not feeling the level of fulfillment you thought you would when this all began.

The choice is yours.

As educators, we go through rigorous preparation to become a teacher, with years of coursework, observation hours, certification exams, student teaching experiences, and so much more, only to get into our own classroom and find out the game is nothing like what we've prepared for. This is especially frustrating because you know you have so much to offer your students, but you always feel five steps behind. As a teacher of teachers, I often hear comments along the lines of, "This is not what I thought it would be…," or "Getting consistent and meaningful participation from students is a constant challenge," or "Helping unmotivated students is my greatest frustration," or even "I just don't feel like I'm making a difference."

Often, we're very good at the technical side of teaching. We know that we should have established rules in our classrooms. We know that we should have routines to promote efficiency with our students and their time. We even know the different learning and psychological theories we're taught in college, and we mastered the concepts of our foundations of education and human growth and development classes in college. All of this only to find out those things alone aren't enough to truly flourish in the classroom of an urban or culturally diverse school.

CREATE A LEARNING ENVIRONMENT THAT HELPS CULTURALLY DIVERSE STUDENTS THRIVE.

I've seen countless instances of educators struggling to break the code and find out what holds their students back. At the beginning of the year, educators are fired up, walking into the classroom chest out and head held high, only to meet swift opposition to every one of their goals. Other times, educators make strong efforts to put new strategies and practices in place, only to get minimal, if any, improvement. This is frustrating to say the least, and often leaves educators feeling like they were wrong: "Maybe this is not the career for me…" or "Maybe I can't make a difference…" I'm here to tell you that you can and you will! I see and have coached educators in what some might consider very difficult situations. I wouldn't be honest if I didn't agree—they are difficult situations—however, that's only when you're unprepared.

With the struggles that can come along with teaching in inner-city and culturally diverse schools, I meet a lot of teachers who've tried one thing after another but cannot seem to make anything happen. Maybe they see a glimpse of success here or there, but nothing that really lasts. I find that these teachers, after putting so much time and effort into trying to improve, give up or get so worn out that they end up in an instructional holding pattern, doing what they've got to do just to get by[2].

A TEACHER WHO IS ABLE TO MOVE THE CLASS IS MASTERFUL AT EFFECTIVELY COMMUNICATING IDEAS AS ONE PERSON TO A CLASSROOM FULL OF PEOPLE.

Truly flourishing in the classroom is about creating the right balance and getting the necessary parts well-represented in your classroom. Think about your favorite song for a moment. Each instrument adds to the song in a different way, with different sounds and different effects on the song as a whole. You take any of those key elements away, and you've created an imbalance that can turn what once was a musical masterpiece into something totally different. But when all parts are there and balanced, the harmony that results from the mix allows us as humans to enjoy the pleasurable sounds of music.

To Move the Class, I'm talking about an educator who is able to transform a collection of learning objectives into an engaging, next-level, cosmic experience for their students. This educator recognizes that it is not a matter of simply getting students to memorize information. A teacher who is able to

Move the Class is masterful at effectively communicating ideas as one person to a classroom full of people, recognizing and responding to behavior patterns, and knowing the class well enough to know what to say and do at all times, in real time. It's a lot, I can admit that.

 ## TRULY FLOURISHING IN THE CLASSROOM IS ABOUT CREATING THE RIGHT BALANCE.

But I'm here to show you that it can be done. As a matter of fact, it is done. Every day in urban classrooms and schools across this country. There are teachers of culturally diverse students who are absolute rock stars in the classroom! I had a guest on episode 4 of my podcast, *Teach Hustle Inspire*, who came into a school and literally in one year's time did the almost unthinkable with her students. It was truly remarkable, to say the least. Teaching in a suburb of Atlanta, Georgia, in a low-income and highly minority area, she increased the pass rate of her students' reading scores by 30 percentage points. Unreal. She got the same students to knock it out of the park in math, too, as every last one of them passed the state math assessments. A 100% pass rate, which was a huge jump from the year before. What happens in those walls and others like hers that produces this against-all-odds magic? How does she do it? Can you learn to do that too? You absolutely can.

A source of stimulation in a one-to-many environment, both the DJ and teacher are artists as they use their catalogue of songs and learning objectives to create an exchange of energy. Both are constantly assessing and adjusting, making moves in real time, all the time. The result is not just another event for the crowd, or another lesson for the class, but an experience. The correlation I discovered between these seemingly very different roles is undeniable. One uses records, the other uses lesson plans.

THE PROFESSOR & THE DJ

CHARACTERISTICS	DJ	TEACHER
MOTIVATOR: THE SOURCE OF STIMULATION OR A REASON TO DO SOMETHING, KEEPS THINGS MOVING	✓	✓
ONE-TO-MANY: ONE PERSON FACILITATING THE EXPERIENCE OF A GROUP OR CROWD	✓	✓
ARTIST: THE PRODUCT OF EXPERIENCE THAT HAS THE INFLUENCE OF SOMEONE'S IMAGINATION OR CREATIVITY	✓	✓
CATALYST: EXCHANGE OF ENERGY. THEY FEED OFF YOU FIRST, THEN YOU FEED OFF OF THEM	✓	✓
REAL TIME: IMPORTANT DECISIONS BASED ON CONTINUAL ASSESSMENTS THAT HAVE TO BE MADE IN REAL TIME, ALL THE TIME	✓	✓
CURATOR: SELECTS AND DECIDES WHAT CONTENT WILL BE PRESENTED AND HOW	✓	✓

You see, a good DJ is a master at specific elements and understands and leverages these elements for crowd enjoyment.

Knowing how to effectively mix these technical elements is also critical to take DJing from playing songs one after the other to creating an experience. Likewise, that is the goal for teaching. We use the elements of urban education to create an educational experience. This experience is not just for our students, but for ourselves as well.

A SOURCE OF STIMULATION IN A ONE-TO-MANY ENVIRONMENT, BOTH THE DJ AND. TEACHER ARE ARTISTS

#MOVETHECLASS

The DJ with two turntables and a mic is a one-person powerhouse whose role is to transform a collection of songs in a crate to an engaging, next-level, cosmic experience for the audience. With this collection of songs, it is not simply a matter of playing songs people like, one after the other. The DJ has to be a master of quite a few different elements to create an ideal experience. We're talking about song selection, blending, transitions, timing, adjusting levels, matching themes, reading and responding to behavior patterns, and knowing the audience well enough to know what to say and what to play at all times and in real time.

This is an artistic display of specific elements that is about the process as much as it is about the outcome. What we're talking about is a process that is nurtured and nourished every step of the way to create an engaging and enjoyable experience to move the crowd. It becomes more than just listening. It elevates to an exchange of energy from DJ to crowd and crowd back to DJ over and over again, one feeding off of the other.

Just the same, a well-equipped educator is also a one-person powerhouse whose role is to transform a collection of learning objectives and lessons into an engaging, next-level, cosmic experience for their students. With this content expertise, it is simply not a matter of getting students to memorize information and terms one after the other. The teacher has to be a master of quite a few different elements to create an ideal experience. We're talking about lesson selection, communication, assessing, adjusting plans, responding to behavior patterns, and knowing the class well enough to know what to say and what to do at all times, in real time.

This is a calculated blend of specific elements that is about the process as much as it is about the outcome. What we're talking about is a process that is nurtured and nourished every step of the way to create an engaging and enjoyable experience to Move the Class. It becomes more than just learning. It elevates to an exchange of energy from teacher to class and class right back to the teacher over and over again, each feeding off of the other.

ACHIEVEMENT

The first element in urban education is all about getting the students from where they are to where they need to be. This challenge can be more than meets the eye, because our African American, Asian American, Latinx, Native American, and low-income students walk into our classrooms at many different levels: some are right on target, some are ahead, some are behind, and some are really, really behind. When it comes to teaching learners from diverse backgrounds, we understand there's a disconnect somewhere. Achievement is all about recognizing that many of the strategies we put in place to help our students achieve, to get them from where they are to where they need be, are only treating the symptoms.

This first critical element puts us in a position to transform learning objectives and tasks that students perceive as mundane or boring into genuinely interesting and engaging experiences. What we've come to learn is that educators with this type of focus are not just successful with students in urban classrooms, but this is the type of teaching that can reach all. Achievement is the first step on your way to Move the Class.

ALLIANCE

How can we not only tell, but show our students that in our classroom, they are welcomed and they are safe? What impactful ways can we communicate to our minority students "I see you" and "You are valued"? Teaching in urban schools, it's all about connecting with our students and creating genuine relationships that build an Alliance.

One of the most common mistakes made teaching in urban schools is that relationships are often left out of the equation. The best educators you'll ever see are able to communicate and motivate different types of people in different types of situations. This is a critical component to Move the Class, as relationship-building with your students establishes the necessary connection needed to impact all other areas of the classroom. Alliance goes beyond persuasion and is nowhere near manipulation. We're talking about genuine relationships that result in students wanting to work harder for both themselves and you.

AWARENESS

The next element focuses on a part of the equation in the classroom that is too often overlooked: the teacher. To Move the Class, we're talking about the whole classroom—the students, the learning environment, and, of course, the teacher. I often work with educators who experience high levels of stress and low motivation, with no real answers as to how to overcome the obstacles that come along with teaching in an urban setting. They end up feeling like too many things are out of their control and perceive these things cannot be dealt with.

Awareness as a tool is extremely powerful because this element hones in on a lot of factors that are often overlooked when it comes to the success of teachers. When I tell you that it is an absolute game-changer, that is no exaggeration. A game-changer.

ARTISTRY

Artistry is all about bringing new and exciting ways of teaching and learning into the classroom. You'll also find that this will rub off on your students in a positive way. You will create new and exciting learning experiences for them, which will foster new and exciting ways for them to demonstrate their knowledge and their ability to solve problems. If you think about it, that's what education does—it prepares us to solve problems. When your students are being taught in new and exciting ways that help them learn, it encourages them to think in new and exciting ways that allow them to demonstrate their individuality to solve and to address problems both in the classroom and in the real world. It's all about how we can leverage our own creative interests in the classroom to really and truly enjoy the art of teaching.

The same way a good DJ is a master at specific elements and understands and leverages these elements for the best experience, a teacher does the same. However, what often happens in our classrooms is teachers are skilled in maybe one of these areas. Even in those instances of initial skill, there is likely still room for growth. And that is ok. Take the element of Alliance, for instance. Perhaps you have had a lot of success with relationship-building with students, but there's an opportunity to step your game up regarding their Achievement. Or perhaps you can come up with creative ideas and lessons, but you never even thought to focus on yourself and develop Awareness of your thoughts, your actions, or those around you. Never has there been (or should there have been) an expectation for perfection. That is ridiculous. But by learning about and developing these areas, you are taking the necessary steps to improve, grow, and absolutely flourish.

To really Move the Class, it starts with a commitment to internalizing these concepts, going beyond simple exposure to each element to having a deeper understanding of—and I might even go so far as to say appreciation for—each element individually. When each element is internalized on an individual level, then we begin to explore ways to create high-level teaching and learning experiences, combining and blending the elements of urban education to establish your role as a *Master of the Mix* in your classroom and school.

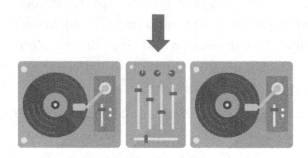

Take a look at the image above. What you have here are the essential elements a DJ uses—two turntables, one on either side of a device called a mixer. The role of the mixer is vital. The device serves as the hub all other devices and sources plug into. It controls what you hear, when you hear it, and at what volume you hear it. The sound that comes into the mixer from each of the turntables is controlled so that there is a perfect balance of each source when and where it is appropriate.

The crossfader at the bottom of the mixer has an important role. The location of the crossfader determines how much you hear of each turntable. Sometimes the crossfader is all the way to the right. Sometimes it is all the way to the left. When it is placed in the middle, you get a perfect blend of everything. What the DJ is doing with the songs, and how the crowd responds, determines what should happen with the crossfader. The DJ uses these levels to mix and create a delicate balance that is consistently nurtured, adjusted, and maintained for the optimum experience. Left unattended, it can be the beginning of a serious, yet completely preventable, struggle.

Becoming a Master of the Mix is all about proficiency in each of the elements of urban education individually, then combining them in ways that work best for you to take your teaching to new levels. Becoming masterful at areas of Achievement is great, but it is simply not enough. Leveraging your abilities in Alliance-building is cool, but that alone won't cut it. Recognizing the importance of Awareness is vital, but by itself, it will not help you flourish. Artistry is about blending the soft science of creativity, but it needs the other elements to even have a chance to live up to its potential. When we recognize and begin to demonstrate that balance, then we begin teaching in a way that truly will Move the Class.

THE ELEMENTS OF URBAN EDUCATION

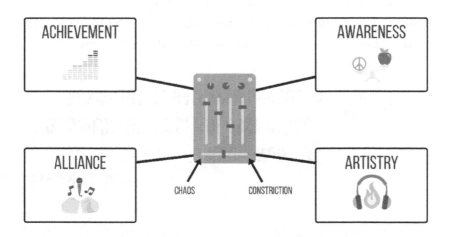

In the classroom, becoming a Master of the Mix is all about the delicate balance of the crossfader. It takes a steady effort to keep the classroom balanced, at that sweet spot right in the center between chaos and constriction. When I refer to chaos in the classroom, I mean a classroom that for whatever reason is in a state of shambles. It emits disorganization; effective discipline does not exist; there is no control; and, of course, there is little to no learning. A classroom in this state often has a direct correlation to the teacher's stress levels, which affects their enjoyment of the profession. Even if the fader isn't all the way to the left in 100% chaos, if it is too far off center too often, these are the situations where teacher burnout is almost inevitable.

When I refer to constriction, I am referring to the crossfader being all the way to the right, a classroom where there is too much control. An environment like this is often rigid, unfriendly, and cold. Discipline is a priority; tension, resentment, and distrust are high. In cases like this, boredom is also common and while the classroom can appear "cooperative" and quiet, it is intellectually oppressive, dimming the students' lights. This is not enjoyable for the students or the teacher.

BECOMING A MASTER OF THE MIX IN YOUR CLASSROOM IS ABOUT INFORMED DECISION-MAKING.

#MOVETHECLASS

You can tell as clear as day when a classroom has a good blend of the elements and when it doesn't. In cases where balance doesn't exist, the environment always results in high levels of stress (for you and your students), students that are unmotivated or disengaged, and a constant power struggle, day in and day out. That type of imbalance is almost palpable. In this book we'll be working to move the crossfader right in the middle and keep it there, creating an integrated, balanced classroom which results in a classroom culture and climate that is electrified with positive energy, learning, and enthusiasm.

"How can I compete with the difficulties my students deal with? What if I have students at different academic levels? What if there are behavior problems? How will this help students learn in my classroom?" When teaching, especially in situations where you're competing against different factors of your students' situations, these are fair questions. Becoming a Master of the Mix in your classroom is about informed decision-making, proactively creating the conditions in which your classroom can best function: adaptability, self-understanding, stronger relationships, and a solid academic foundation. This is an intentional effort that will allow your students, as well as you, to absolutely soar—yes, soar!

When you're a Master of the Mix, you create a balance that is not too far to the left of the fader with chaos, disorganization, and no learning. We also don't want a classroom that is too far to the right of the fader, where we have too much control, constricting the learning environment to the point where it feels cold, rigid, and overly structured. Becoming a Master of the Mix helps you to integrate and balance the various aspects of teaching and flourish in the classroom. The right elements, in the right amount, at the right time, will keep the fader right where it needs to be for maximum flourish in the classroom. What you'll also come to find out is that we use the elements of urban education to create an experience, not only for our students, but for ourselves as well.

I want to help you become a Master of the Mix and show you how to blend the elements together in a way that works for you. Each day, a great deal of things influence the classroom that we have absolutely no control over. However, the good news is that there are actually *more* impactful things we do have influence and control over, which will determine student success in the classroom as well as our own. With your hand always on the crossfader, making adjustments to the levels along the way, we'll get you blending these elements in no time! Are you ready?

End Notes

1. "The Choice is Yours" (Black Sheep, 1991). Mercury/PolyGram

2. "Get By" (Talib Kweli, 2002). Rawkus

TRACK 2

DON'T BELIEVE THE
URBAN EDUCATION HYPE

Recognizing and refocusing the lens

Later in my career as an educator, I decided to continue my quest to be great by becoming a full-time graduate student. This, while still teaching full time, with the added responsibility of a leadership position in my school. One could definitely be led to say I was doing the most—and that's because I was. I was definitely doing the most. But I enjoyed it and felt that I was growing as a person and an educator. That leadership position afforded me the opportunity to understand so much more about the behind-the-scenes part of education. I participated in and facilitated a lot of professional development opportunities, volunteered to head committees, and was in a constant stage of research as I prepared to write my dissertation. Even with all of this, I soon found out that in the world of urban education, I was not as prepared as I needed to be. While teaching a lesson one day, there was a knock at my door. The resulting conversation didn't seem to be a big deal on the surface—an exchange of greetings, followed by a quick signature for some routine teacher paperwork—completely shifted the way I thought about my students. All of them.

I'll get back to exactly what happened after I explain some background details shortly. But first tell me if this sounds familiar: in your path to grow as an educator, you come across a professional development opportunity that seems interesting. You investigate a little more to see what it's all about. The details look good, the topic is relevant to what you need, and so you decide to attend. Cool. During the session, the information that is presented definitely seems of use and you leave pumped and excited, ready to try out these new strategies and techniques in your classroom. The next day, you implement what you learned exactly the way the presenter told you to, but no luck. You don't give up, though. You're too determined for that. New things require adjustments sometimes, no problem. You go back to your notes, re-strategize, and try again. This time, you make a better effort to change your behavior and have a positive attitude about these new techniques and ideas. And to your surprise, you have some success—yes! But still it is moderate success, at best. Since some success is better than no success at all, you stick with it for a while. But the longer you stick with it, the clearer it gets that the change that you had hoped for is not what actually happened. It's not a failure, per se, but it certainly hasn't given you what you needed to make a significant impact on student success in your urban classroom or school. Sound familiar?

THE ISSUE REALLY ISN'T THE ISSUE, THE WAY WE SEE THE ISSUE IS THE REAL ISSUE.

Often, there are instances in multicultural education that teachers are flat-out not ready for. Situations that can arise teaching low-income or students of color become challenges not because something is wrong, but because we are not prepared for them. What I've come to learn, however, is that the issue really isn't the issue, the way we *see* the issue is the real issue.

In many instances, the reason for minimal success when implementing new strategies as a teacher in an urban school is because there are misalignments in the *paradigms* that are needed to be successful in these settings. This misalignment not only inhibits growth, but many times causes regression because it can add to frustration when you've made a solid effort to change your behavior and your attitude for your students' sake.

WHAT IS A PARADIGM?

The good folks at Merriam-Webster define a paradigm as "a philosophical or theoretical framework of any kind." Basically, a paradigm is the perspective through which we view the world around us—including our classroom. The key word in that is our *perspective*, how we as individuals may see it, not necessarily how it actually *is*. Our paradigms represent our perspective and it is from our perspective that we make decisions. That is critical to understand, so much so that I'm going to say it again—*our paradigms represent our perspective and it is from our perspective that we make decisions.*

For example, suppose the workshop you attended focused on instructional strategies. Instructional strategies are, no doubt, an integral part of the learning environment, but how you implement those strategies makes all the difference. If you left that session only to experience minimal success, if that, it is likely that the changes made were one-dimensional. These are changes that, although we hope they do, don't come anywhere close to getting you the results you had hoped for.

While the techniques and strategies you learn at a workshop may be of use to help redirect your behavior in the classroom with intentions of improving student achievement, often it's of little use because that doesn't quite get to the root of the issue. It's almost like spending all day washing, waxing, and polishing a car that has no engine; when it's all said and done, you're still going nowhere. This is not necessarily a character issue, but more a misalignment in paradigms, which makes it easy to create static in a classroom setting.

As Master of the Mix, teaching culturally diverse (and many times traditionally underserved) students requires a strong foundation that goes below the surface. This begins with understanding paradigms. Although paradigms are not often considered for how we can impact and influence our classrooms and students, I challenge you to consider a few things that might allow you to think about this differently moving forward.

Paradigms are the way we see the world and, in this case, our classrooms. Once the paradigms we have and the assumptions that go along with them are formed, unless they are exposed intentionally, they essentially disappear from view. When this happens, not only do we not see or pay attention to our paradigms, we do not question them, either.

UNLESS OUR PARADIGMS ARE ACKNOWLEDGED, THEY REMAIN HIDDEN FROM US AND ARE THEREFORE UNQUESTIONABLE.

Things get kind of tricky when we talk about a positive attitude or even changing your behavior (i.e., "working harder"). This is because without considering our paradigms we are essentially working harder while heading in the wrong direction. A positive attitude and changed behavior are truly surface level and only create small change, in the grand scheme of things. Success at the highest levels requires a fundamental shift in our perspective first. Only then will we begin to see true results. Believe that.

According to the educational data, at this moment it is possible to predict the results you'll have in your classroom or school because you teach students of color. Why? Because when we learn and prepare to become teachers, generally speaking we are taught to teach the numerically dominant population. This is not a bad thing at all, but it puts us in a positon where our skillset may be inadequate for our multicultural classrooms. As a result, many step into situations they are not ready for in urban and culturally diverse schools, which consequently develops a narrative about the students in these schools that isn't always so positive, to say the least.

Unless our paradigms and their associated assumptions about teaching in urban or culturally diverse schools are acknowledged, they remain hidden from us and are therefore unquestionable. Accepting a paradigm shift can be extremely difficult, as, many times, to acknowledge this goes against what we've come to understand about the world around us. Sometimes this can take place over a long period of time, but quite often it can happen in an instant. But believe me when I tell you, on the other side of a paradigm shift lies true accomplishment and game-changing breakthroughs for both you and your students.

For me, this happened when I got that knock at my door which ended up completely shifting the way that I thought about my students. This particular day, my class was finishing up an activity and as I was about to prompt them to wrap things up, there was a knock at the door. A special education teacher entered the room, apologized for the interruption, and asked for my signature for some paperwork to acknowledge one of my student's instructional accommodations. She explained to me that somehow, this particular document had been overlooked earlier in the term when all of the other paperwork was signed for other students. Normally, this information is dispersed at the very beginning of the year, and at this point we were toward the end of the first term—almost nine weeks in.

BECAUSE I HELD THAT STUDENT TO THE SAME STANDARDS AND EXPECTATIONS AS HIS PEERS, HE MET THOSE EXPECTATIONS WITH NO PROBLEM.

When I saw the name of the student for whom the special education accommodations were for, it threw me off. I had to double check with the special education teacher to see if there was a typo because the student she had listed, as far as what I had seen those first nine weeks of the year, did not in any way present himself as struggling or needing any of the accommodations listed on those documents. This student had done every bit of work, participated in all of the discussions, and was in most cases was able to answer or figure out answers we had in our class just the same as the other students.

This was a shock to me as, on one hand, I felt terrible because I clearly had not given the student the accommodations and assistance he may have needed. On the other, I saw that because I held that student to the same standards and expectations as his peers, he met those expectations with no problem. You see, the shock came in that because I did not have the (sometimes) debilitating paradigm of this student being labeled as special education, he performed at the same level as his peers with no problem.

Can you imagine in that moment what I felt? My entire paradigm had shifted, and quickly at that. That brief, but imperative, instance made me realize I had pre-conceived notions about certain students and what they could or could not do. This moment caused me to see things very differently for my students. Now, because I see things differently, I think differently. Because I think differently, I feel differently, and, as a result of all of this, my actions and behaviors now are totally different because they come from a different place. This mindset adjustment caused me to reflect on quite a few things, not the least of which was how many other times I may have, whether consciously or subconsciously, lowered my expectations for my students because they needed any amount of special education accommodations.

To change our paradigms, the first step is to bring them out of the darkness and into the marvelous light and notice them. Acknowledge them, recognize they exist, and take notice. My paradigm shift with the special education documentation allowed me to notice my thinking toward students that may have been previously labeled as needing special education services. It allowed me to see that even though I made efforts to make my classroom inclusive and have equity in my teaching, my actions could have limited their true success and stifled their potential. But not anymore—not in my classroom. My limiting mindset was exposed and I was determined to not let my old assumptions hold me or my students back anymore.

TYPES OF PARADIGMS

When I hear the word paradigm I think perspective, or point of view, you know, how you look at something or someone. What I don't think about is how a paradigm literally affects and impacts everything. Like, every single thing, including how I process information and interpret the world around me. I make decisions based on how I interpret the world around me. I behave based on how I interpret the world around me. And, needless to say, I teach and interact with students based on how I interpret the world around me.

We don't see our students and schools with our eyes, we see them *through* our eyes with cells of recognition in our brain— almost like contact lenses or glasses we wear so regularly that we forget they are there. These cells or lenses in our brain filter what we observe through our personal paradigm, and in turn these become mental programs that guide all of our habitual behavior. All of it. And please believe many of our habitual behaviors make themselves comfortable right in our classrooms. This is because paradigms control creativity and logic, as well as your professional abilities.

Moving the Class begins with the idea of understanding how our paradigms impact our daily lives. We do this by simply taking notice. That's it. Take notice of your paradigms. It's also important to know that there are different kinds of paradigms we may have as it relates to different parts of the classroom. I call these our scholastic paradigms. For example:

Teaching. Our teaching paradigm says students are taught by sitting quietly at their desks while the teacher gives the lesson. In many instances, you stand in front of the classroom and teach the lesson with all eyes on you and everyone focused. Schoolwork is done on your own, and students are assessed to see who was paying attention and who has been learning. If they studied well enough, they'd do well. If they didn't, their grades would reflect so, and would clearly signify a lack of effort of the part of the student. The grades that result from this indicate success and failure.

Cultural. Our cultural paradigm tells us that we're comfortable around people who act and talk like us, people who eat the same things we do and who have similar backgrounds and life experiences as we do. Our cultural paradigm also tells us that the way we do things is the way they should continue to be done.

Urban Education. Our urban education paradigm conveys things like "you should have learned that already" when the culturally diverse or inner-city students don't know something we feel they're supposed to. We do not want to discourage them, so for their sake, with their best interests in mind, we lower the bar a little. Our urban education paradigm also tells us that these students need "fixing" or "saving."

Specifically, your teaching paradigm is likely influenced not only by your own educational experiences, but how you were prepared to become a teacher. We are taught to teach the average student, in the average classroom, in an average school, prepared only to solve average problems. Here's the interesting part about this—"average" doesn't exist. Think about the "average" student in any given grade. No one child fits that description—there's always something that's different. Always. And that's ok! There will always be something different about each and every student you have and, in some cases, a lot of things are different. Sometimes when we step into the classroom, we're simply not prepared.

CHECK YOURSELF BEFORE YOU WRECK YOURSELF[1]

Our scholastic paradigms are shaped by our environment, community, and education. We can only see the world the way we've lived it, and there's nothing wrong with that. Through my life experiences, both good and bad, I learned how to interpret the world around me. Just like through your life experiences, both good and bad, you learned how to interpret the world around you. Without giving conscious thought to paradigms, it's pretty much impossible to view the world any other way. Where we start to run into issues is when the lived experiences of others don't match our own and we begin to interpret the actions (or lack thereof) of other people as needing to be "fixed."

As an example, when we're asked to teach students who aren't performing at the level we think they should be, based on our urban education paradigm, we have the goal to get the most out of our students. We challenge them to give it their all and move educational mountains with the best of intentions. But when we realize that we're up against students that read two or more years below grade level, or students that obviously do not trust you from the moment you step into the classroom and therefore make no attempts to try, we quickly see that some adjustments have to be made. When our best-laid plans go awry, many times the first and seemingly most appropriate thing to do is take a step back and lower the bar a little bit. Perhaps the expectations we've set are just too high, and we need to make more achievable goals for our students. This is justified and it's for their own good, right?

Often, even with a positive attitude, changed behavior, and genuinely good intentions, we find ourselves at an academic dead end, leading to inevitable frustration, stress, and burnout. To remedy this, for the sake of ourselves and our students, we lower our expectations. But lowered expectations only mean one thing—and let me give you a hint, it isn't higher student achievement. What we have to do is learn to step back and examine our paradigms. In other words, check yourself before you wreck yourself.

Again, our paradigms represent our perspective and it is from our perspective that we make decisions. This means that our paradigms have a huge influence in our lives and classrooms. Big changes for dramatic improvement in your classroom are right on the other side of a paradigm shift. But you cannot shift your paradigms until you recognize they exist.

Serving students of color can create a lot of issues for most. But to be real, the problem isn't the problem—the problem is the way we see the problem. In your own reality, it is easy to lose sight of the fact that your personal limitations are not the absolute measure of student success when teaching students of color. There are paths that exist to success beyond what we can immediately see. However, when you fail to recognize the power of your paradigms, but still try to improve, you might as well be trying to plant seeds in concrete because you'll pretty much get the same results.

Now that you consciously take notice of your perspective, you are mindful of the flow of your awareness, and pay attention to your paradigms for what they are. The truth is, your paradigms are in action whether you recognize them or not. You can choose to be a passenger or a driver. A pawn or a player. At the end of the day, the choice is yours.

WHAT WE HAVE TO DO IS LEARN TO STEP BACK AND EXAMINE OUR PARADIGMS. IN OTHER WORDS, CHECK YOURSELF BEFORE YOU WRECK YOURSELF.

As a Master of the Mix, your role is to create an experience like no other in your classroom. You might feel like the odds are stacked against you and it is likely impossible for you to do anything more than just "get by." I'm here to tell you that impossible is one of, if not *the* most incorrectly used word in our language. It has found its way, too commonly, into our everyday language—especially when it comes to teaching in urban schools. Impossible means it cannot be done—no way, no how, forget about it. This book is here to show you how to shift your paradigm in four critical areas, and how this can lay the groundwork for ultimate flourishing in your classroom—for both you and your students. This is where the cycle of change begins. This is where we get downright transformational and start to Move the Class.

End Notes

1. "Check Yo Self" (Ice Cube, 1992). Priority Records

The Track title is a play on the lyrics from "Don't Believe the Hype" (Public Enemy, 1988). Def Jam

TRACK 3

CULTURE RULES EVERYTHING AROUND ME

Using your students' culture to engage them in learning

The narrative promoted around teaching students of color often speaks of the discipline and structure required. The New York Times bestselling author Dr. Christopher Emdin speaks of the unwritten expectations of educators in urban areas to have strong classroom management skills and not be a pushover. This practices are often presented in ways that are veiled as "tough love," which is what these students "need." This promotes a limiting paradigm of these students, what they can do, and who they are as people. Teachers that go into urban and low-income schools wielding these skills as the ones to solve all problems are soon met with resistance like a brick wall. This turns into an environment that is more oppressive than educational. The next thing you know, you have a classroom with an air of resentment, perceived disrespect, and apathy because students feel their values and needs are being ignored. At a fundamental level, some of the ways many teachers are prepared to be educators clash with the skills needed to teach in urban schools because culture is simply not a part of the conversation the way it needs to be.

True achievement starts with a high focus on classroom engagement. Engagement is an outcome of **motivation,** which is an outcome of what we value, which is an outcome of—believe it or not—our culture. Culture has a tremendous impact on how we learn, and when this is not considered, it is pretty much a guessing game as to whether or not a lesson will be successful. Often the tendency is to use traditional teaching practices that focus on memorization, as well as individual worksheets or assignments. It's a safe bet to claim these things won't promote true engagement and achievement because they do not take advantage of diverse student cultures, and therefore have little relevance to the students. In other words, without giving consideration to your students' culture, success of lessons taught in a classroom are basically a gamble.

 ## ENGAGEMENT IS AN OUTCOME OF OUR CULTURE.

#MOVETHECLASS

From the student's perspective, there are norms and rules in place that everyone should understand and abide by. Instead, a teacher, although well-intentioned, comes in to the game trying to change everything the students know about it. Their culture and its importance are diminished. It doesn't feel right to students on a fundamental level, and many times, beyond being uncomfortable, it can feel offensive and disrespectful. This is because our personal cultures carry unspoken rules of what is considered courteous, acceptable social interaction, appropriate personal space, and so much more. Social violations of these types are deeply rooted into our emotions and offenses here are a one-way ticket to mistrust, instant levels of stress, and social tension. Students in these situations actively choose not to participate, become behavior concerns, or do their work because they're supposed to, but are really not happy about it at all.

A MISUNDERSTANDING

How can a lack of tapping into our students' culture prove to be a problem? I'm glad you asked—let me show you how a singular vocabulary misunderstanding can be enough to make it appear as though students know less than they really do. For example, completing some practice questions to prepare for a standardized test one year, students were asked to solve a word problem.

17   The Johnsons want to replace some furniture in their home. In order to shop for the right size, they need to know the furniture measurements.

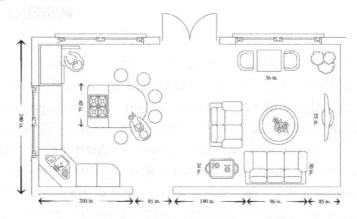

Find the perimeter of the Johnson's sofa to help them shop for another.

For this particular practice question the students were asked to find the perimeter of the sofa. As with any word problem, there's a certain amount of background knowledge that is needed to get the correct answer. In this case, knowing that to find the perimeter, you add up the length and width of all sides is the most important thing. Or is it?

At first glance, it was a little puzzling as to why this was so difficult for the students. Was it because they forgot the rules for calculating an object's perimeter? Were they simply adding wrong?

What actually threw these students off was that the term "sofa" was unfamiliar to them. Because of this, they weren't sure what to measure. The term more familiar to these students and used in their homes was "couch." Realizing this and making a quick substitution for the word, the lightbulb went off and a collective "oh!" was heard. With this simple connection, the students were able to correctly answer the question. What would have easily been interpreted as these students being inadequate intellectually was actually a matter of two culturally different words used to describe the same thing.

THERE ARE LEVELS TO THIS[1]

Culture is basically a set of unwritten rules that are always in play. It doesn't matter where you come from, your race, or your ethnicity, you have some sort of culture that has shaped you and the people around you. Slang students use, their customary behaviors, foods they eat, their beliefs, and even how they dress, are all a part of our students' culture. This is important to students because it not only represents them, it *is* them. The way they give a friend a pound, or greet someone, the way they wear their hats, or even the music they listen to are all integral parts of who they are. Teachers who take the time to not only be aware of these things but embrace them realize it is advantageous.

However, this often is where it stops. Many times, even after attempts to bring their students' culture into the classroom or school, teachers feel their efforts yield minimal results, if any at all. This is because many efforts that attempt to acknowledge student culture only tap into what educational researcher Zaretta Hammond calls surface culture.

We recognize our students' customs, slang, foods, beliefs, and dress, and make efforts to acknowledge and embrace these things about them. However, these are merely the observable parts of culture. You see the tip of the iceberg, when there is so much more beneath the surface. Culture is what feels "normal" to us and is shaped by unwritten social habits that expose themselves in everything we do. With this understanding, we have to bring light to the fact that culture impacts identity, which impacts behavior, which impacts how students respond to their teachers in the classroom. Without understanding this, we create a cultural gap that limits success in the classroom.

 ## CULTURE IS BASICALLY A SET OF UNWRITTEN RULES THAT ARE ALWAYS IN PLAY.

One of the ways we can begin to close this gap is first to acknowledge that understanding our students' culture is critical in order to Move the Class. Culture is unwritten and often difficult to define and describe from person to person, but it impacts literally everything we do. When we have an understanding of our students' culture below the surface, we can begin to tap into ways to teach and reach each of them.

Mr. Mike Brown was a guest on the 9th episode of my podcast, *Teach Hustle Inspire*. In this episode, he explains how he realized the cultural differences between he and his students was a barrier to his success. Realizing this, he explains the steps he took to bridge this gap:

"The teachers need to spend more time in the community that they serve. And here's the caveat to that. It's not 'I'm the teacher' where they're introduced as the teacher, because they are there [even outside of the classroom] in a [proverbial] superior role. But I'm talking about just participating in the community as a community member. Which means that you are there to observe, you are there to absorb, you are there to be a part of the culture. Not to be a high representative that steps into the culture only to step right back out just to say, 'I was there and I saw you,' but as an active participant in that community."

There is so much power in that statement because I can think of countless times where we interact with our students outside of the classroom, and it's inevitable that to some extent we are still in that role of the teacher, that authoritative position. What Mr. Brown is saying is that instead, when we engage in the community outside of the classroom, we should step out of that role and just be a regular participant. Absorb what's happening around you. That's it.

 **CULTURE IS WHAT FEELS "NORMAL" TO US AND IS SHAPED BY UNWRITTEN SOCIAL HABITS THAT EXPOSE THEMSELVES IN EVERYTHING WE DO.**

He goes on to say, "I started getting my car fixed in the neighborhood, I started going grocery shopping in the neighborhood, I started banking in the neighborhood, and what you realize is when you go there, the bank tellers are their parents. When you're relying on their [your students'] parents to do your banking, you no longer think that you have this intellectual property [or superiority] over them. Because you realize in their profession, 'I need them…'"

Mr. Brown goes on to say how he further immersed himself in his students' community by going to the dentist there. A dentist who was, you guessed it, a student's parent. Not only did this contribute to a huge shift in his paradigm about his students, but it allowed him to see and experience firsthand his students' culture to be a better educator. Was he able to Move the Class? Oh, he most definitely was.

Effective teaching in urban classrooms connects the content to the students' backgrounds in meaningful ways, below the surface levels of culture. In this specific example, Mr. Brown was experiencing his students' shallow culture. Shallow culture is the unspoken, unwritten rules that exist around your regular, everyday interactions with people. This defines the rules for friendship, personal space, eye contact, appropriate touching, concepts of time, what is considered courteous, and so much more. It's at this level of culture that nonverbal communication either builds or blocks trust. Shallow culture is rooted in emotion, so violations of any kind at this level cause problems very, very quickly.

"But I don't mean to be offensive to my students, I really don't!" Of course you don't. But as a Master of the Mix in your classroom, it is imperative you know what makes your students tick, how they think, and why they think that way, and leverage this to catapult your teaching something serious! That is the way we close the cultural gap, which paves the way for us to have better relationships, learning experiences, and so much more. Mr. Brown taking the time to intentionally bear witness to and learn the daily happenings of his students' community as a participant outside his role allowed him to take in these unwritten rules of shallow culture, facilitating his paradigm shift and improving his skills as an educator.

To Move the Class, we're talking about teaching where "the how," "the what," and "the why" of learning are not only unified, but meaningful and fun. Students in urban and multicultural schools need to be taught in ways that accommodate their unique mix of race, ethnicity, class, and community, while contributing to their everyday cultural identity. Educating students in this manner teaches *to* and *through* their personal and intellectual capabilities, setting them up for authentic success. This is where we go even further below surface and shallow culture and tap into deep culture.

MOVE THE CLASS - TEACHING WHERE "THE HOW," "THE WHAT," AND "THE WHY" OF LEARNING ARE MEANINGFUL.

A person's deep culture is in control of how he or she learns and processes new information. Culture at this depth has an intense emotional connection to trust because it is here where we determine whether something is a threat or a reward. Any and all challenges to someone's deep culture immediately produce cultural shock, if you will, and trigger that person's fight-or-flight response. Deep culture is just that—it's deep. It's comprised of tacit knowledge and assumptions that guide how we see and perceive everything. Everything!

CHURCH. TABERNACLE. PREACH.

As an example, for many Black students in inner-city and suburban communities, church has a strong cultural and community significance. Whether in attendance because you generally want to be there, or because grandma makes you go, many of us find ourselves on a church pew Sunday mornings. As a matter of fact, often it was more times than that. What's not always so obvious about these worship experiences is that we are there to learn. In its own way, church is a classroom. The topic of focus is spiritual, but you're learning nonetheless. The biggest difference between a church and a classroom is the atmosphere.

Often, you can hear what's going on before you even get to the church door. The organist, drummer, and other musicians provide a soundtrack to the atmosphere (the DJ) and the pastor or worship leader stands in the front with a mic in their hands (the MC), engaging the congregation in a way that welcomes their participation and energy from those fortunate enough to be in the number.

THE MC IS STRUCTURED IN THEIR APPROACH, BUT AD LIBS AND FREELY FLOWS WITH A PURPOSE IN MIND.

Dr. Christopher Emdin explains how the style in which the black church teaches and engages can be a valuable framework to use in school classrooms. When the pastor speaks to the audience, there is an air of invitation to participate, to be a part of what is going on. There are instances when the pastor repeats words or phrases with changes in volume and emphasis as if to say, "You obviously didn't hear me. Let me say it again so that I can get the response I'm looking for and make sure you're engaged." It works every time. When emotion, volume changes, and repetition are added to what is being said, it invites the members to not merely listen, but actively participate.

Many times in church, the sermon given (the lesson, if you will), includes a generous mix of biblical text, current events, and social commentary, all in the spirit of grounding the lesson and new material (the sermon) in what the audience members already know and can relate to (current events and social commentary). Often smooth and almost free-flowing, the sermons are delivered in a carefully balanced way. They have a defined structure, but allow room for improvisation.

Similarly, when an MC is on the mic in front of a crowd, it is his or her job to create, harness, and perpetuate the energy, like the church preacher. They stand in front of the audience, taking in and giving right back the energy that is transferred between them like an electrical circuit. The MC is structured in their approach, but ad libs and freely flows with a specific purpose in mind. More importantly, the MC's demeanor and words demand crowd participation, so much so that one is absolutely compelled to oblige. With emotion, conviction, and enthusiasm, the MC calls out:

Just throw your hands in the air

And wave 'em like you just don't care!

And if you're not a square

From Delaware,

And you got on clean underwear,

Somebody say, "Oh yeah!"[2]

The crowd inevitably responds with an emphatic, "Oh yeah!" Works every time.

End Notes

1. Levels" (Meek Mill, 2013). MMG/Atlantic
2. "The Roof is on Fire" (Rock Master Scott & The Dynamic Three, 1984). Priority Records

The Track title is a play on the lyrics from "C.R.E.A.M. (Cash Rules Everything Around Me)" (Wu-Tang Clan, 1994). Loud Records

SIDE A INTERLUDE

BACK IN THE DAY WHEN I WAS YOUNG

Figuring out that what you need, you may already have

Back in the '90s, early in my high school days, I, like most kids, wanted to be fly. Anyone can tell you that as an adolescent youth, your appearance means so much—perhaps too much sometimes, but it is extremely important nonetheless. Growing up in New York, it was all about sneakers and clothes. This was when Michael Jordan was still playing basketball and his shoes were the hottest thing to come off the presses every year. I didn't have money for all of that, so I had to figure out another way. At that time, in my eyes, to help propel me to superior levels of flyness, I needed my hair to be dope. My barber was great. He was masterful with the clippers and could fade my hair like no other. In times when I was feeling extra bold, he cut all sorts of creative designs and parts in my hair. I loved every bit of it. But I was getting to the point where it was time for a change. I needed an upgrade, if you will, and for me that meant I needed an S-Curl.

I would walk through the aisles of Pathmark and make my way to the hair-care aisle, see that blue and silver box and imagine all the possibilities. In order for that to happen, there was a very intense chemical process that would literally change the texture of my natural hair, but I did not care. I went so far as to buy it, take it home, and ask my mother would she put in my S-Curl for me. I was met with a swift and resounding "no."

My dreams shattered before they got off the ground. I began to ask for patience, because I knew that as soon as I got out of that house as an adult I was going to have my S-Curl, but I had a long way to go. I seriously prayed for the Lord to give me peace in my journey, to wait on Thee and be happy with my tapered mini-fro in the meantime. Now, you have to remember, I was about 14 at the time, so again this was a big deal. But alas, my struggle went on for two years. That blue and gray box began to deteriorate to a faded picture of what could've been. This whole time I tried and tried to persuade my mom. She still wasn't having it. Her reasoning was that it could mess up my scalp, damage my hair, and end up doing more harm than good. But my foolish 14-year-old self couldn't see beyond what I wanted right then and there.

Until one day, I came across a kid at my school who had the S-Curl of life, walking down the hall with his hair absolutely flourishing. With a tone of admiration, I explained my desire for an S-Curl and asked him how the process was and if it burned his skin. But to my surprise he told me he didn't have an S-Curl. Enter instant shock. He told me he was using a simple hair gel called *Pro-Styl*. He said, "You should try it—might work for you, too." That particular product was a dark gel made for culturally diverse hair textures—like mine. At that moment I would've ran out of school if I didn't think it would lead to swift disciplinary action. But as soon as that bell rang, I went right to CVS, found my way to their hair-care section and picked up this mysterious brown gel. I went home, applied a dollop to my mini-fro, laid down my edges, and right before my eyes my hair curled up. Come to find out, that gel served as a small catalyst to activate my God-given hair flourish—this whole time I *already had* everything I needed.

Don't miss the message here, my friend…

Here you are, willing to chemically straighten the edges of your life, thinking you've got to break it down to build it back up to achieve your goals. You've been told "no" for reasons you can't understand, but continue to try to press your way down a path you don't need to take. In your shortsightedness, you can't see this resistance is to protect you from damage, heartache, and strife. I am here to tell you, you don't need to go down that road because you already have what you need! The Good Lord gave you the talents and knowledge to flourish already, from right where you are—you just have to activate them. I didn't need that S-Curl box because I already had the Lord's S-Curl, and so do you! So get that book or that coach, take that course or listen to that podcast, and use that as the catalyst to activate what you *already have*!

End Notes

The Side A Interlude title is from the lyrics to "Back in the Day" (Ahmad, 1994). Giants/Warner Bros Records

SIDE B
THE ELEMENTS

TRACK 4

ACHIEVEMENT - AND IF YOU DON'T KNOW, NOW YOU PEDAGOGICALLY KNOW

*Getting your students from where they are
to where they need to be*

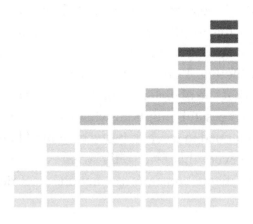

Let me tell you about a teacher I had the chance to work with. As a school building leader, part of my role was to observe teachers and provide feedback to support their growth as professionals. I know how intimidating this can be, so I like to give a heads-up when I can, especially in the case of teachers that may be new to the building or profession as a whole. The teacher I was set to observe on this particular day was new to the building, but had teaching experience, and knew her content like the back of her hand.

She was a short in stature, soft-spoken and reserved. This could have been due to the fact that she was new to the school, but maybe it was just her nature. I was not concerned as I've seen plenty of instances where the most unsuspecting educators you will ever see walk in and command the classroom like being on the mic was second nature. So I reserved judgment until I had seen her in action.

In our prior discussions of trying to help her acclimate to the building, I was able to tell she enjoyed teaching and was looking forward to our school. When it came to our discussion of her lesson plans, though, I grew a bit concerned because I wasn't quite sure if what she planned would work. I wasn't seeing how she could be successful with both what she was going to teach and how she planned to teach it, based on what I knew about the students. However, this was only what was on paper and sometimes the magic comes in the action, so, I decided, let it rock.

Well…

About 10 or 15 minutes into the lesson, I walked in, trying not to interrupt the groove—but there was no groove. There was a lot going on. Not a lot going on as in different engaging activities across the room, but a lot going on as far as downright disorganization and confusion. Some students were up and walking around, some were talking, others sat at their desks because they didn't know what else to do. Although she didn't say it verbally, her facial expression said, "help me…please!"

We got her through the lesson, and afterward took a few moments to discuss what happened. I wanted to first let her know that she didn't have anything to worry about and this wouldn't reflect negatively on her performance or evaluation. I was there strictly to help. In our follow-up discussion, it was easy for me to tell that although she had prior teaching experience, and knew her content like the back of her hand, there was a critical element missing. You might be thinking, this is a classic case of lack of classroom management skills. However, I'd like to challenge you to think a little differently about this. The missing element is small enough to often be overlooked, but large enough to have your classroom in absolute shambles if ignored.

There is a strong narrative around the achievement of students from diverse backgrounds. It is often highlighted how students of color and those that come from low-income communities underperform compared to white students. This has come to be known as the achievement gap. What we know is that this gap among students actually starts small and gets wider as the students move from grade to grade. As early as kindergarten, students are seen as underperforming on some level, but as they move up in grade, they can never quite catch up and are always at least two steps behind.

What you're seeing in these instances are actually large misunderstandings of how students of color achieve. As a result of these misunderstandings, often, more intellectually challenging tasks are delayed, if given at all, until it is felt that these students are "ready." This continual focus on less challenging tasks, while most times is an effort to offer some sense of achievement for students, actually hinders progress because they are not being challenged. You're left with a cycle of lower-level activities that continue year after year after year. As these same students get older, they have not been taught the skills necessary to think critically, problem solve, or synthesize knowledge the way they need to, and the achievement gap pretty much widens itself.

WHAT YOU'RE SEEING IN THESE INSTANCES ARE ACTUALLY LARGE MISUNDERSTANDINGS OF HOW STUDENTS OF COLOR ACHIEVE.

It is obvious there is cause for concern in how we teach our multicultural students. I wholeheartedly believe many educators recognize the value of culture and bringing it into the classroom. What's not so obvious, however, is how to do that.

Imagine this: it's the coldest winter ever. Short days, freezing temperatures, and downright blustery conditions. Everyone stays indoors to avoid the harsh outdoor conditions, but this creates the perfect storm for sneezed-in hands to touch one person after another and spread all kinds of germs.

Now you've got the flu.

The flu is not fun. Like, at all. As you experience body aches, fatigue, a sore throat, and a cough to match, you're miserable and find your way to the doctor. This sickness, this debilitating force that has taken over your body needs to be treated. Fast. Imagine yourself at the doctor. You present your case to your doctor, and it is confirmed there is definitely a problem. As an attempt to resolve the issue, you're prescribed some medicine to give you some relief and hopefully solve the whole problem. The medicine you're prescribed? Cough drops.

"That should do it," says the doctor. And you commence, even in your sickness, to look at him with a look of bewilderment. Not antibiotics, pain medication, or antiviral medications to prevent complications or shorten the severity of this sickness. You get cough drops. Immediate frustration and anger set in. You know good and well that some cough drops will not in any way help you in this condition. Those *might*, in an off chance, help pacify the symptoms of a sore throat, maybe, but in no way will they treat the source of the problem or prevent it from getting worse.

When we see our students of color not performing well on assessments or getting low grades, we dig through our educator crates attempting to make adjustments and get the train back on the tracks. In most cases, we review and re-teach the information or provide extra help. Yet we get results with minimal, if any, improvement. Here again, the flu is being treated with cough drops.

Is it that urban or culturally diverse students are not intellectually capable? Is it safe to assume that entire groups are not capable? If you look at what the broad educational data say, the answer is yes.

When students step into our classroom, generally speaking, our goal for them is achievement—to take their learning from where it is to where it needs to be.

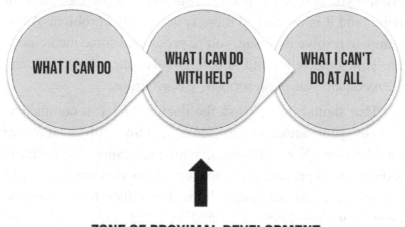

ZONE OF PROXIMAL DEVELOPMENT

This space, which bridges what a student can do by his or herself and what the student cannot yet do without support is where the focus of our instruction lies. In that space, the teacher controls the elements and ideas that are just beyond the students' ability, gradually increasing expectations as they are ushered from one concept to the next, building on the students' newly acquired knowledge. Throughout the learning process, student support is gradually adjusted and released until the student becomes an independent learner. Ideally, what the student is able to do with the help of the teacher today, they'll be able to do themselves tomorrow. Only that's not what happens. Often, what the child does with the help of the teacher today, they still need the help of the teacher for tomorrow. And the day after that. And the day after that.

As educators, when it comes to learners from diverse backgrounds, we understand there's a disconnect somewhere. However, what we often don't realize is that many of the strategies we put in place to help our students achieve, to get them from where they are to where they need be, are only treating the symptoms—the needle is no longer in the groove of the record. Teaching our students from diverse backgrounds in ways that don't match how they understand the world around them directly relates to the deficiencies in learning highlighted in the data. But in these instances when the train goes off the track, we have to use the right methods to pick it up, pick it up, pick it up!

Talking to a lot of teachers of diverse learners, I often hear comments such as:

"It just seems they don't want to learn..."

"I am struggling to find ways to get my students engaged in what we're learning."

"I just can't seem to reach them..."

"There's no interest or even concern from my students about school."

I, too, had similar thoughts. For example, I recall many instances of trying to get my students to learn critical vocabulary terms. Terms they needed to know, or else it was almost pointless to move forward. I would do things such as write the terms on the board, and have students practice each term's spelling, look up the definition, and, of course, use it in a sentence. I was teaching the way I was taught. It seemed natural to do the same exact thing.

In a perfect world, these new vocabulary words become a part of the students' daily conversation around the classroom to demonstrate their understanding and reinforce what they've learned. Only that's not what happened. They almost never used the new words in conversation around the classroom. If they did, it was likely in the wrong context. I can easily recall each of these vocabulary lessons as riddled with yawning and/or bare minimum engagement in the learning. I curated a classroom environment that could honestly be labeled as boring. With that, it was pretty predictable that when they were tested later in the week on these definitions, results were consistently mediocre at best.

But I held on to the belief that if I could get my students to fully and genuinely engage, it would make a big difference in their achievement. I would often wonder, were the students not applying themselves? Were the words too difficult? Am I just not that good of a teacher yet? There's got to be something I'm missing here. And there was.

What adds to this frustration of not knowing what to do is when you see or know of another teacher that, with students from the same exact population as yours, has these miraculous test scores, high levels of engagement, and very few discipline problems, and the students love her. Somehow, she was able to get her students to beat the odds and has the numbers to back it up. What's difference in the walls of those classrooms and how can it be replicated?

ENGAGEMENT IS KEY

We try to encourage our students to work their hardest for good grades, recognition, or participation in special clubs and programs. These things are so common and built into the fabric of school that it is almost unheard of to think in other ways about these foundational structures. Let me help you out here—the reason these things are not nearly enough to Move the Class is because they're each based off external "carrot-and-stick" types of motivation.

Have you ever told a student if s/he doesn't work hard, they won't get a good grade, and they don't seem concerned in the slightest? Is it that they don't want to learn or they don't care about school? No, that's actually far from the truth. The idea of grades, test scores, GPAs, and the like merely communicates the idea of reward and punishment. While this is a common practice and can be successful for some students, for many students from diverse cultural backgrounds this is a direct cause for resentment and conflict because the idea of reward and punishment with that carrot-and-stick framework reinforces manipulation. Should grades and GPAs be ignored? Absolutely not. But it is so important to know these things should not be used as a way to motivate your audience to engage.

Achievement for your students of color starts with high levels of classroom engagement. As mentioned in Track 3, engagement is an outcome of **motivation,** which is an outcome of what we value, which is an outcome of culture. Many do not consider the tremendous impact culture has on how we learn. I promise you your diverse students care very much about learning and school—when it makes sense to them. This means the how, why, and what of the content they're learning must be meaningful.

As an educator, it can be frustrating to try different things to help your students achieve and not get you the results you've hoped for. We spend countless hours planning, strategizing, and analyzing data, only to barely move the academic needle. But, having a solid understanding of what hasn't worked in the past to engage your students allows you to be more intentional about how your students will be able to achieve in the future. Knowing this, and *why* these tactics haven't worked is exciting because now we start to get some clarity as to what has kept us from being able to Move the Class.

Wielding the power of two turntables and a mic, any DJ that you see will also have a collection of music in what are known as crates. These are exactly what they sound like—those plastic crates that grocery stores use to transport and store milk were also used to carry and store records. These crates become a collection for DJs, as they hold any and all music that can be used to move the crowd. Now, with advancements in technology, a DJ's crates are digital, stored on the hard drive of a computer. As a DJ works, the search from song to song is known as digging in the crates. When a DJ digs in the crates, the goal is to find the right song or set of songs to convey a musical message and transform a song from an isolated track to a larger fabric of songs, creating an experience.

As educators, when we Move the Class, we dig into the crates with the goal of transforming normally mundane learning objectives and tasks into learning experiences by making them culturally relevant. We do this by creating learning experiences that mimic our students' own cultural learning tools so that learning fits right into their natural way of processing information. Educators that teach in ways that are culturally responsive soon recognize that teaching this way is helpful for all students, not just students of color.

Designing learning experiences for students that are culturally responsive has several key components: **Connection**, **Alignment**, and **Value**. The opportunity for **Connection** allows students to work cooperatively with and rely on one another. Especially for diverse learners, this function is a part of the social fabric of these students' daily lives. Bringing Connection into the classroom on a regular basis helps to promote a sense of community and synergy.

Alignment in learning happens through the way content is taught. For example, gamifying learning experiences, providing opportunities for repetition, solving puzzles, creating relationships between things that appear seemingly unrelated, and especially utilizing story. These methods are effective as they tap into and align with students of color's cultural learning style.

EDUCATORS THAT TEACH IN WAYS THAT ARE CULTURALLY RESPONSIVE SOON RECOGNIZE THAT TEACHING THIS WAY IS HELPFUL FOR ALL STUDENTS.

Value is created through experiences that thoughtfully incorporate students' intrinsic significance and perspective. This is done by creating an environment where both the students and teacher feel respected by and connected to one another *and* the work. This creates a classroom with a favorable disposition toward learning, fueling maximum effort toward challenges at all levels.

When creating learning experiences that leverage Connection, Alignment, and Value, the big idea you do not want to miss is consistency. Too often, educators may attempt to engage their students with these strategies, but in ways that are inconsistent. Then, when the desired results are not achieved, the ideas are altogether scrapped and the educator goes back to what is familiar and comfortable, teaching from within their own paradigms. Consistency in Connection, Alignment, and Value is the best thing you can do to promote that next-level engagement for diverse learners in your classroom.

CLOSING THE ATTITUDE GAP

Student buy-in is a critical component to increase their willingness to learn. Bringing their everyday lives into the classroom opens up a world of possibilities as students begin to see how what they are learning relates to what they've experienced in their lives. However, there are certainly instances when it is not that easy. Teaching in urban schools, educating students from all sorts of situations can be emotionally taxing when students in our classrooms seem to simply go through the motions. Making the effort day after day without any results can feel we're fighting an uphill battle.

So many of our students have faced so many challenges for so long, be it academic, personal, or both, that sometimes they don't have the will to want to put any effort into achieving at all. I like how bestselling author Principal Baruti Kafele sums up how we can begin to approach not just closing the achievement gap, but also what he has coined the attitude gap. The definition of the attitude gap is "the gap between those students who have the *will* to achieve excellence and those who do not."

In our classrooms, we have those students that are high-flyers. Regardless of the task, they can take it. If they can't handle it, they'll take the initiative on their own to solve the problem, and before long they are off and running, ready for the next challenge. Then you have your students who are right on target, right where they need to be. These are your students who consistently have to make an effort in order to stay afloat, but that effort is there and one way or another, with good teaching, they can get the job done. Then you have your students who struggle all the way around for one reason or another, and in many instances appear like they don't care. These students seemingly have no ambition, no goals, no purpose, no motivation—they are just there. These are the students who do not possess the will to want to achieve and demonstrate excellence. But please believe me when I tell you there is greatness within those students—I know it, and I am positive you do, too. There is brilliance behind that eye roll, there is genius under that hat, there is high-level intellect just below the surface of that attitude. It's there.

THERE IS BRILLIANCE BEHIND THAT EYE ROLL, THERE IS GENIUS UNDER THAT HAT.
#MOVETHECLASS

Principal Kafele asks, "What do we have in place to tap into our students' greatness?" "How can we ourselves as educators tap into our students' greatest abilities?" Educators who demonstrate—and that word is important: demonstrate—a relentless belief in our students, matched with learning experiences that embody Connection, Alignment, and Value, Move the Class. By our actions and the learning environment we intentionally create, we communicate relentlessly on a conscious and subconscious level to our students, "I like you, I believe in you, I love you, I value you, I appreciate you, I understand you, I empathize with you, and I care about you." This is how we begin to close the attitude gap, and this is how even our most challenging students can excel in the area of Achievement.

KNOW YOUR AUDIENCE

When you know your audience, and teach in ways that are culturally responsive, it helps to take the pressure off of you and can greatly reduce some of the frustrations of teaching. As educators, we want the best for our students and make great efforts to teach, motivate, and push our students in any and every way we can think of. However, even with our best efforts, it can be difficult to get the results you'd hope for. Doing this day in and day out, time and time again, inevitably leads to burnout and frustration. Frustration that no one wants to deal with, and, fortunately, no one has to. Teaching that is culturally responsive helps alleviate some of the pressure because it creates teaching that is teacher-student cooperative. Every day shouldn't and doesn't have to be an uphill battle—absolutely not!

Teaching that makes a difference in the lives of students of color finds ways to connect school to the students' everyday lives, every day. Like your favorite remixed song, it's a perfect blend of out-of-school and community learning with new classroom learning. When we leverage the culture of our African American, Asian American, Latinx, and Native American students, we cultivate their strengths, increasing engagement, and therefore increasing their achievement. I want to make sure you understand what I'm saying here. Teaching in ways that are culturally responsive doesn't mean you need to become a competitor on "You Got Served" and dance your way through the periodic table, or pick up a mic and rap through the parts of speech. Not at all. There is nothing at all wrong with bringing dance and rhyme into the classroom, as these methods are fun and certainly get the attention of your students. But what I want to be clear on is that these ideas are, in many ways, still surface, and can be difficult to sustain. Culturally responsive teaching is far more than this.

TEACHING THAT MAKES A DIFFERENCE IN THE LIVES OF STUDENTS OF COLOR FINDS WAYS TO CONNECT SCHOOL TO THE STUDENTS' EVERYDAY LIVES, EVERY DAY.
#MOVETHECLASS

When we teach in ways that are culturally responsive, although extremely important, it's not so much about racial and ethnic pride as it is about helping our diverse learners make sense of new learning in ways that imitate their cultural learning styles. This is teaching in a way that reflects how your diverse learners' mom, dad, grandparents, family, and community taught them, years before they ever stepped foot inside of a school building. These ideas of Connection, Alignment, and Value were not explicitly taught to your culturally diverse students; they are already a part of who they are. It is a part of their everyday lives because it is in their homes and communities, and a part of their regular social interactions.

The goal here is to know your audience, to understand how we can teach in ways that match our students' ways of understanding and interacting with the world. When we do this, we teach in ways that are culturally responsive.

WHEN YOU CONNECT WITH THEM IN WAYS THAT THEY FEEL ARE AUTHENTIC, YOU CAN TRULY MOVE MOUNTAINS.

Often, efforts to bring culture into the classroom are done at a surface level. For instance, a teacher takes an existing lesson and adds Mexico, Africa, or hip-hop to the conversation. If this becomes a situation that doesn't get the results they had hoped for, it's easy to decide that bringing culture into the classroom doesn't work. And now we're back at square one.

Culture is not discussed at an in-depth level as we prepare to become educators, when it's actually one of the biggest factors in how you can connect with your students. When you connect with them in ways that they feel are authentic, you can truly move mountains. While culture is often defined and perceived by schools as the celebration of important people, religions, traditions, and holidays, as well as an appreciation of the customs of different groups, it is so much more than that. Your students' culture has everything to do with who they are and how they learn. Because of this, teaching students with instruction that taps into shallow and deep culture is where the magic happens.

HOW DO WE DO THIS?

There are so many different avenues that you can use to bring what the students experience into the classroom in a positive and effective manner. I found that I struggled a lot with engagement when I did not make a connection to the lived experiences of my students. Often, we try to teach students new material based *only* on what they've already learned academically, when we should also be leveraging what they've *experienced* culturally. When these connections to their experiences are made, it gets exciting because you can almost see the synapses in their brains fire as they make correlations. This is at the root of what it means to bring culture into the classroom to enhance learning: bringing students' everyday lives into the classroom every day.

This opens up a world of possibilities as students begin to see how what they are learning relates to what they experience outside of school. And it gives this learning new meaning and purpose.

At its surface, this can seem intimidating. You may be thinking, "Well, I don't know anything about my students' lives outside of the classroom," or "I cannot relate to my students lives outside of the classroom." This mindset can keep you from an awesome opportunity to dive deeper to get to learn these things about your students. Just like Mr. Mike Brown mentioned in Track 3, this has so many benefits, none the least of which are establishing better relationships with your students and leveraging this information to help them learn more.

If you have not already discovered this, many students are eager to share about what is happening in their lives. They are natural chatterboxes. How you use this information will vary day to day and lesson to lesson, but the point is to be intentional about using this information to your advantage for the sake of relating to your students and helping them achieve. You may also be surprised to find out how much they may connect to something in your own life as you dig deeper. Sharing these commonalities and experiences can prove to be so fruitful in so many ways in your students' learning; there's a connection for them *and* for you.

WHEN ENGAGED WITH LESSONS AND LEARNING THAT GIVES CONSIDERATION TO CULTURE, WE'RE LITERALLY CHANGING THE GAME.

Plenty of evidence backs up the fact that culturally responsive teaching strengthens the student's connection to school and affects how well your multicultural learners achieve. When engaged with lessons and learning that gives consideration to culture, we're literally changing the game. We're talking about moving from learning where the student is dependent on the teacher and is a passive bystander in the classroom to where the student develops habits that promote higher-level, independent thinking and actively participates in the learning process for the sake of learning.

When a DJ knows the audience, they create crowd experiences that are visibly enjoyable through great song selection and energy given and received from the crowd. This exchange of energy happens because they are enjoying themselves as a result of you! They are smiling, dancing, and feeling good because of you.

As a teacher, knowing your audience and how they best achieve is not only beneficial for them and their academic and personal interests, but yours as well. When you know your audience and can intentionally design learning experiences that bring out the best in your students each day, you become more confident and comfortable in what you're doing as an educator in every way! When you know your audience and understand how leveraging culture results in true achievement, an exchange of energy is also present. They are smiling, engaging, and feeling good because of you. Some of the most invigorating moments for educators happen when they witness student "ah-ha" moments, when they say, "I get it!" Those moments send a surge of energy through you that can only be compared to lightning. They're enjoying learning, and you're enjoying that they're enjoying learning all at the same time.

WHEN YOU KNOW YOUR AUDIENCE YOU BECOME MORE CONFIDENT AND COMFORTABLE AS AN EDUCATOR.

When we don't focus on Achievement with learning that is culturally responsive, without even realizing it, we end up stifling their potential. We've got to be more careful with engagement that leverages external reward and punishment factors simply because that's what we're used to. Don't forget how important it is to challenge your existing paradigms. The teaching paradigm we often hold says that if our students paid attention and studied well enough, they'd do well. If they didn't, their grades would reflect this, indicating success or failure. Teaching that does not give consideration to the culture of students in urban or multicultural schools promotes mediocrity at best, as well as students who depend *only* on you to learn.

AUTHENTIC LEARNING FOR DIVERSE LEARNERS IS LEARNING THAT SPEAKS TO WHAT THEY INTRINSICALLY VALUE.

When learning to become an educator, we take classes to understand the foundations of education and learn about education theories, all of which are important, but we are not taught specifically enough about teaching students of color, plain and simple. The lack of understanding culture creates a lack of understanding of how to effectively engage a large number of your students. When we teach in ways that are relevant culturally, we invite the opportunity to tap into the natural ability of all of our students, regardless of their past experiences or current circumstances.

Authentic learning for diverse learners is learning that speaks to what they intrinsically value. Many lessons and teaching strategies can have too much of a focus on those things that only hold weight as a means of the carrot-and-stick, external rewards or punishments. However, true achievement is the result of learning that is fueled internally. By cultivating intrinsic motivation, we speak to the values of diverse learners because what they're being taught, how it is presented, and why they're learning it means something to them.

End Notes

The Track title is a play on the lyrics from "Juicy" (Notorious B.I.G., 1994). Bad Boy Records

TRACK 5

ALLIANCE - ME AND YOU, YOUR MAMA AND YOUR STUDENTS TOO

Relationship-building in multicultural schools

In the music studio one day, likely taking a break from recording, six men engaged in a verbal exchange of ideas. Except, this exchange of ideas took place over a bed a music. Hip-hop music, to be exact. These men created a cypher. In hip-hop, the cypher refers to a group of people improvising rap lyrics, usually over a hip-hop instrumental, but sometimes without one. In the same way jazz musicians will take turns and improvise over a steady groove, feeding off of the energy of one another, rappers can build off one another vocally. I cannot even begin to tell you the level of difficulty that is involved with having to think so fast on your feet, while staying on beat, and in line with the chosen topic.

 THE FIST BUMP IS SO POWERFUL IN THE CLASSROOM BECAUSE IT HARNESSES THE POWER OF TOUCH.

On this particular day, the beat is playing on a continuous loop in the background and the men have circled up to listen and flow with the beat. There is an air of excitement and anticipation as the beat vibes through the speakers. The participants are nodding their heads, smiling, and leaning in and out, back and forth to the beat. One at a time, each takes the role as the MC. The last participant casually bops into the middle to take stage and close out the cypher, rapping about the chosen topic.

Today's subject: soda.

> "I give a pound to my man with my right hand
> 'Cause I, I keep the Sprite in the left hand and I
> Push the button when I don't wanna hear nothin'

I let it go when I wanna hear something
This is how we flow
When we in the studio
Freestyle with Sprite yo how the rest go?
First things first
obey your thirst
Sprite, alright?"[1]

In 1995, Pete Rock, C.L. Smooth, Grand Puba, and a host of others were a part of a legendary commercial that to this day I think needs to be put back on television because it was one of the coolest, most authentic, and creative commercials in my lifetime. In the last segment, Grand Puba, smoothly and casually strolls to the middle, while giving his cypher neighbor an effortless, yet significant, pound.

 ## TOUCH AS A CONNECTION MECHANISM CONVEYS COMPASSION AND ASKS FOR TRUST, A CRITICAL FACTOR IN CREATING A GENUINE ALLIANCE.

The fist bump, aka the pound, aka the dap, and other high fives and handshake methods are so powerful in the classroom because they harness the power of touch. Touch as a connection mechanism conveys compassion and asks for trust, a critical factor in creating a genuine Alliance.

We want our students to be their authentic selves in our classrooms. Exchanges such as these help create an environment that invites participation and communicates, on an emotional level, "you can trust me."

In that exchange, whether you recognize it or not, a lot is said. Through these gestures, we tell our students they are welcomed, they are safe, and that we are here to help them learn and grow. Whether used as a morning greeting, a sign of approval, or affirmation of a job well done, these exchanges, especially the fist bump, are examples of things that hold significant cultural weight for many students of color. To Move the Class, it is important to connect with students in as many ways as possible. Creating an opportunity for a genuine fist bump with your students will go a long way to establishing and reinforcing the Alliance that is critical in urban and culturally diverse schools.

 ## TEACHING IS NOT A STERILE, TACTICAL PROFESSION. TEACHING IS RELATIONAL.

Teaching is not a sterile, tactical profession. Teaching is relational. A good educator has to be able to relate to communicate and motivate different types of people in different types of situations, and this requires the ability to build relationships. In a given circumstance, a good teacher has to be able to step back, assess what is happening, and make important decisions in that moment based on what they notice. In DJ terms, the teacher has to choose the right record.

Approaching teaching in a tactical, regimented, impersonal way is almost the same thing as a DJ simply pushing the start button for a pre-designated playlist. A good DJ has to constantly move off of the feedback provided by the audience. You learn to read the crowd and move accordingly. If it were a matter of simply pushing play, one would be able to determine a set playlist at home, arrange the songs in a specific order, and simply play one after the other without giving it a second thought. This comes off as cold and disconnected. It doesn't feel personal or welcoming and has an immediate impact on the flow of everything that is happening at that time. Yes, the songs selected may be popular, but in a social environment where you're trying to harness the energy of many, it's all about timing and presentation. So that means you might have to look back and dig into the crates to find the perfect tune to match the crowd's energy, in order to take them from where they are to where you want them to be. It takes time to build the skills to recognize what you're seeing, how to interpret it, and how to leverage that energy.

The same applies with teaching. Good teaching goes beyond the tactical transactions to leveraging the power of relationships to teach. Especially in urban settings with higher populations of minority and/or low-income students, relationships are everything. Everything? Yes, absolutely everything.

I recall many instances of being on the other side of cold and tactical teaching. One teacher I had taught social studies with the use of packets. Just packets of worksheets. One packet each week, packet after packet after packet. We were given the lifeless collections of paper on a weekly basis to complete a certain number of pages per day. Frankly, I don't know how this wasn't seen as a violation of environmental law with the amount of paper that was wasted.

Rarely would there be an opportunity for interaction in this classroom, and this, as I'm sure you can imagine, was an environment with low engagement. The information may have been good, but I'll never know because it wasn't presented in a way that piqued my interest in any way, shape, or form. I wondered sometimes if it was just me. Perhaps teaching with the use of packets would work for some. Maybe I needed to work on becoming a better student. But as I looked around day to day and week to week and month to month, the faces of my classmates told me they felt the exact same way.

In our classrooms, we want to create optimal learning conditions for our students. What we're trying to do is create a productive learning environment, where we the students are involved in classroom activities. When you're on top of your game, classroom rules and procedures are explained day one, and that conversation continues at least throughout the first few weeks. This is the priority during this time because this is where we set the tone for what will take place going forward. Lay the groundwork upfront.

IN URBAN SETTINGS WITH HIGHER POPULATIONS OF MINORITY AND/OR LOW-INCOME STUDENTS, RELATIONSHIPS ARE EVERYTHING.

In urban schools, these types of tactics are just the beginning. While important, real strides to Move the Class come when teachers have authentic relationships with their students, when there is an Alliance. It is a proven fact that the best educators you will ever see have solid relationships with their students. Actually, that statement is so important I'll say it again. *The best educators you will ever see have solid relationships with their students.* And the secret sauce to a great student-teacher Alliance begins with two essential ingredients: trust and communication. One of the reasons I was able to almost instantaneously deal with Jonathan in the story from the introduction is because I had established an Alliance. I can show you exactly how you can do the same.

TRUST

Often, trust is thought of as how much you can count on someone to hold your deepest, darkest secrets and never tell another soul. While this is true, allow me to show you another side of trust and how this is interpreted by your students. Your students trust you when your *ask* aligns with your *actions*.

 YOUR STUDENTS TRUST YOU WHEN YOUR ASK ALIGNS WITH YOUR ACTIONS.

Imagine a building administrator talking to the school staff. This conversation revolves around some of the basic rules of professionalism, highlighting the importance of being prepared each day, ready to teach, and of course being on time—the usual. But the next morning, that person walks into the building late. You take notice but think nothing of it at first, until it happens the next day, and maybe even a few more times after that. As a leader, this person is communicating on a subconscious level that following the rules is not that important; that person's actions do not align with their ask. As a result, it becomes easy to say to yourself, "Shoot, if an administrator doesn't have to be on time, neither do I!" when you're running late. The next time, there's even less effort on your part to be on time. Pretty soon, you're walking into the building late with a fresh cup of coffee, wishing someone would say something to you for being late.

In this instance, that administrator is asking you to follow a different set of rules. Their *ask* doesn't align with their *actions*. Because of the administrator's lack of integrity in following their own rules, a level of distrust results, not only making it easy for you to get lax on the rules yourself, but also to question their overall commitment and competency in that position, because these things are all related. Your students look at you the same way.

I recall an instance from when I first started teaching. The school had a strict "no cell phones" rule. But that was just for students, right? Of course it was. While students were in the middle of an activity, I'd take out my phone and respond to messages, catch up on the group, because, again, that rule is for students, right? Similarly to the previous scenario, I didn't realize I was breaching my students' trust by telling them to follow a different set of rules than I did. It led to some problems that could have completely been avoided, wasting valuable learning time on more than one occasion, all because I failed to understand trust.

Many of us were raised in an environment where it was said or at least implied to "do as I say, not as I do." But that old adage never held a child back from imitating the behaviors they see;

that is how they learn. So when they saw me use my phone, they figured it was ok to use theirs. Truly leading by example would have been displaying the behaviors I want them to display. My *ask* should have aligned with my *actions*.

When a student doesn't trust what you say, regardless of your intent, they don't process the information in the way that it was meant to be delivered. Lack of trust from a student triples the time it takes to complete a task or learning objective. *Triples.* Even if what you're telling them has their absolute best interest in mind, they process your message as manipulation if they don't trust you. When that feeling of "this teacher is trying to manipulate and take advantage of me" shows up, the student goes into a state of self-protection. When a student functions out of this state, which is rooted in fear, focus that could be used for learning is now used for self-defense. And as you can imagine, trying to reach, let alone *teach*, a defensive student is not an easy task. Not at all.

However, when that trust level is high, when you've established that Alliance with deposits of integrity and genuine interest in that student's well-being (personally and academically), you have the ability to reach that student when others cannot. Not only can you reach that student, but because that barrier is down, you have the opportunity to teach that student as well. They'll want to do better—for themselves and for you.

COMMUNICATION

As an added bonus, when trust is high, communication is so much easier and much more effective. But think about this first.

If there were boxes that said "overall very positive" or "overall very negative," which could be checked to describe your communication with some of your more difficult students? You might be surprised if you were to actually tally the number of positive comments versus the number of negative comments what the outcome may be. Or, let's face it, you may not be surprised at all.

In urban schools, where students are more likely to deal with situations the likes of which some couldn't even begin to imagine, communication at any level can be a challenge. But the balance in your positive versus negative communication has an incredibly large impact on the overall relationship you have with a student. Positive reinforcement has, without a doubt, been proven to be one of the most effective means for creating Alliances with students. The problem occurs when negative reinforcement outweighs the positive reinforcement, when you react more often to what has gone wrong than proactively encouraging a student when he/she is doing something right.

WHEN THAT TRUST LEVEL IS HIGH YOU HAVE THE ABILITY TO REACH THAT STUDENT WHEN OTHERS CANNOT.

#MOVETHECLASS

Has this ever happened—you tell a student "great job!" and genuinely mean it, but they just sit there and stare at you, without responding at all? In instances of imbalanced communication, where negative comments outweigh the positive, whenever there actually is a good comment or bit a feedback offered, it literally holds no weight. Why? Because that student doesn't have any reason to believe you're not trying to manipulate him/her.

In that student's mind (important point here, in that student's mind), they're being manipulated. If almost everything up until this point has been some sort of corrective feedback telling them what they're doing wrong, or how they need to do this or that better, why in this isolated instance should something positive make them feel good? Psychologically speaking, it takes it takes seven positive comments to outweigh the effects of just one negative comment. That's a 7:1 ratio, which can be extremely difficult to catch up on when there's a deficit.

Also, think about the effect that negative comments can have on a person. Words can literally act like poison because the power of our words is far too often underestimated. Think about that time you wore that new shirt, just as confident as you wanted to be because you know the shirt was nice. A friend comes along and gives you an awkward look followed by words like "What made you wear that shirt?" Said jokingly, and not even coming from a place of shade, those words, a few short phrases said in passing, were enough to have you doubt every wardrobe decision you made that morning. That fast, those words poisoned your thoughts, had you feeling self-conscious, and likely changed your entire mood after that. This is a simple example, but the same holds true for your communication with students, especially if that negative feedback has to do with their behavior or school work. Both are very personal because they speak to their identity and intellect. Negative words hurt and hold a lot of weight, seven times more than something that could have been said that was positive.

> **Pro-tip:** If you know a particular student has an interest in sports team, ask that student what their thoughts are of the last game. If you know another student likes to watch America's Got Talent or The Voice, ask who their favorite contestant is and what they think it'll take for that person to win. Every bit of conversation doesn't have to be about business (school).

Take a look at this and see if you can figure out what's missing from this illustration of communication types:

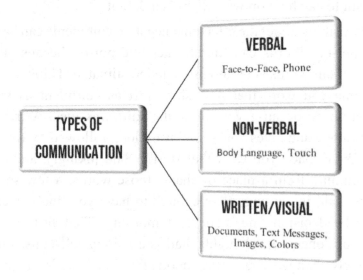

LISTENING

As far as communication we're taught to speak and we're taught to write, but we're never really taught how to listen. Listening is a skill, yes, a skill, whose development all too often goes ignored. Listening is treated as a passive byproduct of communication, where we simply wait for our turn to talk. For many situations of casual conversation, that is all that's needed. But for students in your classrooms who enter the door sometimes with the world on their shoulders, they need more than passive listening skills. Additionally, a quick way to destroy an Alliance that you've work so hard to build is not to really listen to your students.

How often do we passively "hear" the words of our students at a surface level? We get just enough information to begin to formulate what we're going to say as a response. But the next thing we know, the conversation now gets an eye roll or reluctant compliance, all because the student felt like they were not listened to. Next-level communication that will Move the Class requires you to go beyond hearing to masterful listening that is attuned and adept, with the ability to maximize every interaction.

Teaching students of culturally diverse backgrounds, we have to be cognizant of not just how we hear, but how we *listen*. We must be aware. When on the phone, beyond listening to the words we hear, we pick up on key things that give us more information about the conversation. We notice changes in tone that convey emotion, we pick up on the speed of what is being said, which can tell us a lot about the excitement or urgency of the conversation. We can even sense pressure behind words— talking with a clenched jaw, hard or soft vocal inflections, these all give us details as to how to receive what we're given in the conversation. There are many ways information is received and we process it all. We are aware.

Good listening skills are measured by what we do with this awareness. At a basic level, our awareness is focused on ourselves. Yes, we hear the words spoken, but our attention is on what these words mean to us personally. In these types of conversations with your students, the focus lies on "me": my thoughts, my judgments, my feelings, and my conclusions about what is being said. Listening at this level is an important first step, but where we make the mistake is limiting our awareness to this basic level.

TEACHING STUDENTS OF CULTURALLY DIVERSE BACKGROUNDS, WE HAVE TO BE COGNIZANT OF NOT JUST HOW WE HEAR, BUT HOW WE LISTEN.

#MOVETHECLASS

At an advanced level of listening, the focus is acutely on the other. We are not exclusively attached to our personal thoughts and agenda because our focus is occupied by the student who needs us to listen. In this position, we're not trying to figure out what we're going say next or how we can poke holes in their argument. Rather, in that moment, you are aware of what the student is saying and what it means. You're listening for words and the meanings beneath the words. You're listening for expressions and emotions, noticing not only what they say, but what they don't say. You identify—does their body language match what is being said? What emotions are behind the words coming out of their mouth? When you do respond, your response is chosen carefully. And, when listening at this level you pay attention to how the feedback or response is received more than choosing the words you say.

Because it is so rare, if you are an educator who listens with intent and awareness that is focused on your students, you are already leaps and bounds ahead of others who may not be able to connect with their students. You're in a great position to forge a dynamic and mutually beneficial Alliance.

IT'S A TWO-WAY STREET

Another big part of communication is the fact that it works two ways; the way we give communication and the way we receive it. This continues the discussion about culture, where different words or actions mean different things to different people. For example, in my classroom I recall a particular instance where the students were engaged in group activities in different parts of the room. Each person in the group had a specific task and I could tell the students were active in their participation from the noise that could be heard throughout the room. It was good noise.

This particular day, I had to ask a student, Lisa, a question about her work from the day before. So while the students were working, I called out, "Excuse me, Lisa..." She replied "What..?"

Here's where things almost went wrong, quickly. Let me introduce you to Calvin and Monica, my parents. Since before I can remember, growing up in Calvin and Monica's house, there were certain things that were not to be said and done in their presence. Certain words, even though not necessarily "bad words," were considered disrespectful. The word "what," when used as a single-word response, was one of those words. It was made clear on many occasions that when asked a question I was not to respond with "what." In instances where my memory failed me and I would respond to a question from one of my parents like that, there were usually consequences I had to deal with. So, naturally, I took that same message into adulthood and into my classroom.

So in this situation, when I called out to Lisa and she responded "what," I was immediately triggered. In a matter of less than a half of a second, all sorts of responses came flooding into my thoughts:

Who does she think she's talking to?

She clearly forgot where she was.

What did I do to ever give my students a reason to disrespect me?

She's got the wrong one today!

In my mind, for that half a second's worth of time, I went into defense mode. I became culturally reactive to this student (in my mind) to protect myself from losing control. For that brief moment, this perceived disrespect told me I was no longer recognized as an authority in the classroom. Fortunately, before I let those thoughts spew out of my head, I had the wherewithal to pull back on the reins and calm myself down. I was self-aware enough to recognize how the message was actually delivered. When the student responded to me, she did not respond by rolling her eyes, yelling, or anything else that could lead me to believe she was intentionally trying to be disrespectful. While it may seem like an exaggerations, that is how our minds work. We have to be self-aware enough to recognize that communication is a two-way street in how it is given as well as how it is received.

SPREAD LOVE IT'S THE BROOKLYN WAY[2]

When considering student-teacher relationships, you must consider your audience. Not all, but a significant portion of students from urban or low-income neighborhoods, because of circumstances beyond their control, come from homes with a lower level of stability. These students crave strong relationships with you because relationships are a legitimate biological need. Demonstrating love and compassion for your students translates to stronger academic achievement because of its impact on the hippocampus region of the brain. This part of the brain is responsible for learning, memory, and emotional regulation. Take notice that the word "demonstrate" was used for showing love. Many students in our classrooms have swirling thoughts of "Does anyone care about me? Am I loved? Do I matter?" You can care deeply for your students and have a great deal of compassion for them on the inside, but unless you are intentional about demonstrating this so that students can see, hear, and feel the love, they may never know.

 RELATIONSHIPS ARE A LEGITIMATE BIOLOGICAL NEED.

The teacher-student Alliance is a skill that you will learn to master over time. It's all about understanding yourself first, which in turn helps you to better understand others around you.

If you recall from our discussion of becoming a Master of the Mix, it takes consistent effort to balance the classroom. We want to maintain an environment that's not too brash, rigid, and strict, but not out of control, either. Our hand is always on the crossfader and adjusting the levels to keep everything in harmony. Having that genuine Alliance with your students allows you to balance between these two extremes because you'll develop the intuition to know how to respond to certain students in certain situations.

A RELATIONAL CONNECTION BETWEEN A TEACHER AND HIS OR HER STUDENTS IS THE FOUNDATION TO STUDENT ACHIEVEMENT.

A relational connection between a teacher and his or her students is the foundation to student achievement. As you develop the skills of relational teaching, you will learn what proverbial songs to play or records to choose at any given moment. You will develop the ability to know whether or not a lesson is going well, *during* the lesson, making the necessary adjustments on the fly, as opposed to afterward when it may be too late. You'll be the teacher that your students want to work hard for. And when your students come across concepts and ideas with which they struggle, they will put forth that extra effort with your help and encouragement. This adds to making learning more purposeful for your students.

Teachers who connect with their students and have firm relationships find that their students experience less stress, have fewer behavior concerns, and are genuinely more excited about learning. The research shows that the biggest impact on achievement in the classroom is not the class ratio, issues of financial status, or even the identified academic abilities of the students. It is the teacher. These are facts.

As an added bonus, not only will having a strong Alliance with your students prove valuable in helping them behave better on a regular basis, but in instances when there is an inevitable behavior issue, and please believe there will be, the student is much more likely to willfully accept any consequences for their actions.

"Sorry, Ms. Johnson, I shouldn't have done that. I know I have to (insert any logical consequence) now…" Because you've established that relationship, there is more than enough mutual respect to accept and abide by the consequences given, because s/he knows and believes you have his/her best interest in mind.

BE PATIENT

The difficult part about this is that we have to remember laying a foundation of trust and communication to build relationships takes time. We live in a world where almost everything is instant. We can instantly download and read a book, send a message and get a response, and find out the latest news and gossip literally as it is happening.

These days, there is very little reason to wait. While these conveniences save us a lot of time, they have also conditioned us to expect these same results in ways that are simply not possible: primarily with building human relationships. A good educator must know there are no instantaneous genuine relationships. Building a good relationship with a student, especially with students who come from difficult circumstances, takes time. But I promise you, it is time well spent.

After you've laid that foundation of trust and communication to establish a solid Alliance, and student behavior and effort is all the way up, that's when teaching is really fun! Don't forget the benefits of an Alliance work both ways. Not only do your students benefit because they feel valued, want to work harder, and do better, but *you* feel better because it inevitably reduces stress while providing an opportunity for you to increase student achievement with minimal barriers—a legit win-win.

End Notes

1. "Obey Your Thirst" (Grand Puba, CL Smooth, Large Professor, 1995) Sprite Commercial

2. "Juicy" (Notorious B.I.G., 1994). Bad Boy Records

The Track title is a play on the lyrics from "Elevators" (Outkast, 1996). LaFace Records

TRACK 6

AWARENESS - I GOT 99 PROBLEMS
BUT SELF-CARE AIN'T ONE

Self-awareness & self-care
for higher motivation & lower stress

Regardless of what is going on inside or outside of your classroom, what you do have control of every single time is how you respond. There were countless circumstances where I would let the fact that I did not like what a student said to me or the feedback that I got from an observation or email from a parent, have an impact on my emotions, which inevitably impacts what I do and how I interact with my students in the classroom.

It is easy to become a victim of your circumstances and let external things dictate how you feel. Too often, we let factors outside of our control have an influence on how we feel. While you may not have control over what's happening around you, you have every bit of control over how it affects you. This starts with understanding that you do have control.

Awareness of this level of control was exciting because it allowed me the opportunity to step back and think of specific circumstances where I would have an entire lesson, class day, or more ruined over my reaction to something. Through some serious self-reflection, reading, and opportunities for growth, I began to notice that the only person who could impact how I felt was me. If anything else had an effect on how I was feeling, that was because I let it have an effect on how I was feeling. Becoming aware of this presented an opportunity for me to pivot going forward. Now when I receive a piece of news, information, or feedback that I may not like or agree with, I am able to manage its impact on my emotions. This certainly was not an easy action at first, but the fact of me simply recognizing that something was having an impact on how I felt was a tremendous step forward because it allowed me to be aware of my reactions, which allowed me now to focus my energy on getting back to a place of good vibes and energy.

When DJing, if a set didn't go right, I could step back afterward and examine what I had done. I'd take a look at the songs I played, go over how the crowd responded, what would have been a better choice. Now, if an interaction with a student didn't quite go the way I wanted it to, or a lesson didn't quite go as planned, I was able to step back, self-reflect, and recalibrate my energy so next time that lesson or student interaction would be better. That's the biggest lesson—to recognize what caused it and to make it better the next time. There is always going to be an opportunity to make it better, and it is important to take advantage of that notion. Looking forward to how the next time could be better helps improve your mood in that moment, too.

With some consistency, over time I was able to better consciously position myself to feel good more often because I was aware of the things around me and the type of impact that they could have if I let them. This allows me to step back and recalibrate myself when needed and examine the situation to change the results.

Awareness and self-reflection have a huge influence on our emotional state, and everything to do with how we react and interact with ourselves, students, and others around us. Reaching a certain level of emotional intelligence is real game-changer, because recognizing and being able to appropriately react to human emotions, including your own, is a completely underrated skill.

Developing this skill is so important because it reflects how well we apply knowledge and adapt to immediate encounters with others. Emotional intelligence doesn't get enough respect, as we often place too much value on the academic side of education. But what good is knowing the Pythagorean theorem forward and backward if you're not aware enough to recognize the reason students may not want to connect with you in the first place to learn it?

RECOGNIZING AND BEING ABLE TO APPROPRIATELY REACT TO HUMAN EMOTIONS, INCLUDING YOUR OWN, IS A COMPLETELY UNDERRATED SKILL.

Building solid student relationships that transcend academics is about fundamentally understanding both sides of the equation: your students and yourself. I'm talking about the interpersonal side of relationship-building, how well you understand others, what moves them, how they work, and how to work together cooperatively. I'm also talking about turning the mirror on yourself and understanding the *intra*personal side, having the ability to access, recognize, and even discern your own feelings and emotions. As a Master of the Mix, you must learn to monitor and adjust the levels of your ever-changing and highly influential emotions. You can be in control, or you can let them control you.

A Master of the Mix seamlessly blends Awareness and Alliance. Awareness has a strong relationship to Alliance in the sense that every interaction with students can be placed on a spectrum that labels an encounter anywhere from nourishing to toxic. The results are rather simple: the more nourishing the encounter, the more likely the student is to connect with you. The more toxic the encounter, the more likely the student is to shut down, disconnect, and even retaliate in some kind of way.

Every interaction, every conversation, every time you talk to or talk at a student, can be plotted on that spectrum of nourishing to toxic. The idea is to demonstrate Awareness of your interactions so your encounters with students are nourishing.

BUILDING SOLID RELATIONSHIPS IS ABOUT UNDERSTANDING BOTH SIDES OF THE EQUATION: YOUR STUDENTS AND YOURSELF.

#MOVETHECLASS

Often when situations arise in our classrooms, we go straight to evaluating the other person's mood or actions without considering our own. We have to be aware enough to recognize our feelings and emotions as they happen, adjusting the levels and sliding the fader in that moment. It's the difference between getting caught up in the rise of emotions from something that has angered you and having the reflexive thought of, "Ok, this is definitely anger I am feeling right now," even while you're still upset. When you have the ability to be aware of your mood and your thoughts about your mood, you have the ability, at a metacognitive level, to almost step outside of yourself to evaluate what is happening and allow yourself more control in that moment to self-regulate, now in a better position to foster an Alliance because of your Awareness.

When we are more self-aware and can identify what's going on emotionally within us, we are in a better position to read the emotions and feelings of our students. Human emotions are rarely put into words. This is especially true for our students, who, depending on their age, might not even have the vocabulary to verbalize their emotions. But the information is given to us in a great deal of other ways that we can learn to read, even amidst an all-out emotional rollercoaster, through development of our social attunement. Some signs are easy to pick up on, some not so much. It gets easier over time, though—trust me.

SELF-CARE: EATING AND EXERCISE

I believe there's a strong misconception that while teaching students of color, you have to entirely sacrifice yourself in order to have any level of success. The idea instead should not be self-sacrifice, but Awareness of self-care. As educators, we consistently pour into the lives of others, but in order to be successful at this, we have to remember to pour into ourselves first. *First!* While this may come off as being selfish, in fact it is not. We cannot be our best selves for our students when we have high levels of stress, low energy, or low motivation. It's like trying to get water from an empty well. It should be reassuring to know that it is okay to treat ourselves, to relax and recalibrate. Again, this is not selfish because the goal is to be at your best for others.

How can you be at your best? There are a great deal of things that contribute to our overall feeling, many that we are not even aware of. For example, our physical health. While this book is not about diet and fitness, it is important to note that your health outside of the classroom has a significant impact on what you're able to do inside the classroom.

I was shocked to find out how much what I ate affected what I was able to do in the classroom. I love Chinese food and I would eat it all the time if I could. As a matter of fact, I'm almost ashamed to admit how much I ate Chinese food. To save myself some embarrassment, I won't even tell you how much. Just know it was a lot. While I enjoyed the taste and variety of Chinese food, I ignored its impact on my body, which was impacting my mind, which was impacting my teaching. The high levels of sodium and fat content in my beloved Chinese food were legitimately stunting my growth as an educator.

AS EDUCATORS, WE CONSISTENTLY POUR INTO THE LIVES OF OTHERS, BUT TO BE SUCCESSFUL WE HAVE TO REMEMBER TO POUR INTO OURSELVES FIRST.

#MOVETHECLASS

When I realized the impact my diet had on my overall health and my growth as an educator, I began to make some serious changes. Here is where my relationship with my smoothie machine begin. I cut back on the frequency of Chinese food and incorporated more whole foods as a regular part of my diet. Because I was substituting whole, natural foods for shrimp-fried rice, my body reacted differently to what I ate, in a very good way. I had more energy, I was less fatigued, and, more importantly, I felt better. And when I felt better, I thought better. When I thought better, I taught better.

Exercise was also vital to my transformation as an educator because of something I took full advantage of: endorphins.

When I realized the benefits of regular exercise and how it would allow me to sustain higher levels of energy for longer periods of time, I recognized the significant impact exercise could have on what I was able to do in the classroom. I made a consistent effort to exercise at least twice a week. Yes, there were many, many other things I had going on in life, but I felt that it was important for me to be my best, first for myself, and second for my students. Let me tell you, it was well worth it. I began to notice that after completing an exercise routine I would initially be fatigued from the workout, but as my body begin to recuperate, along with my changes in eating, I often found myself feeling great. Not only did this help during and immediately after exercise, but this now allowed me to rest better, which allowed me to wake up with more energy and a clear mind. Do you know how invigorating it can be to Move the Class when you're in a state of high, vibrational energy from those endorphins? It's so dope. It really is!

Awareness of how my health impacted my teaching positioned me to go into the classroom fully present on a regular basis to be at my best for my students. Now, I am not saying that I became a health guru and threw out all of my Doritos. That is far from the truth. But I am saying regular exercise and better eating made a significant impact on what I was able to do for myself, which made a significant impact on what I was able to do for my students.

I also have come to learn that just like internal Awareness has its place, external Awareness also has an important place. As materialistic as it sounds, I firmly believe that if you look good, you feel good! Why? It's probably rooted in some form of narcissism, but who cares. The fact of the matter is that it matters. You and I both know that when you put on that fresh new outfit, or have a fresh haircut or fresh hairdo, you feel good. Fashion is one of those areas where we can be our most creative selves and let our personalities shine. I feel my style is a part of who I am and I take pride in it. I'm sure you do, too.

In my building, I was notorious for bright shirts and socks and I absolutely loved it. They were always eye-catching and, more importantly, they reflected me. There were so many different possibilities and combinations, and socks were an inexpensive way to express myself while being the best teacher I could be in my classroom. My students loved to see what socks I had on each day and would never hesitate when they liked what I was wearing to let me know. "Mr. Woodly, I like your socks today!" Other educators did the same with their own collection of socks or even scarves. I've seen some scarf collections that were out of this world and so fly! Be it socks, scarves, or anything else, accessories are inexpensive and can be so much fun to add to an outfit. When it came to fashion and bright colors, I was being me and I was comfortable and did not shy away from expressing myself in my classroom, but this was certainly not how I started.

When I first began teaching, I was 22 years old and a bit insecure in my abilities. I wanted to make sure that I was presenting my best self. Every day for two years, I wore a full suit. I'm talking button-down shirt, slacks, dress shoes, jacket, and tie. Always. For two years. I was young, but it was imperative to me that I did not appear immature or incapable to hold my own in the classroom. My third year of teaching, I began to relax a little bit and let more of my personality shine in what I wore. I changed the jacket to a simple button-down shirt with a tie. I eventually let the tie go and added a pair of argyle socks once or twice a week. This went on for some time, and as

I got more comfortable, my unusual socks and shirts became an almost daily occurrence. When I came down the hallway, you were going to see me whether you wanted to or not!

At the end of the day, my fashion choices helped me to be more comfortable with who I was as an educator, which subsequently allowed me to reach more students, contributing to higher levels of student engagement and achievement. It took a while, but I had to bring me—all of me—into my classroom. Awareness of this helped me to put forth my best teaching. An unexpected bonus was when my students began to show me their own bright socks, which they wore because I wore them. Someone running into the classroom and pulling up their pant leg to show me their outrageously colored socks would make my day every time!

BLENDING AWARENESS AND ALLIANCE

Relationship-building opportunities are all around you—but you have to open your eyes and see them. Something as simple and seemingly insignificant as socks were a bridge to connect with my students. It took me by surprise when I first started to see students walk into my classroom and show me some bright, eye-catching socks they were wearing that reflected their personalities and interests. It helped strengthen my Awareness of the fact that students are always looking for a way to connect when the opportunity presents itself, but *the opportunity has to present itself.* Now I'm not telling you to run out and purchase a pair of neon yellow highlighter socks. What I am saying is to look for not-so-obvious ways to connect with your students and those around you— it's not always in the way that you might think.

RELATIONSHIP-BUILDING OPPORTUNITIES ARE ALL AROUND YOU— BUT YOU HAVE TO OPEN YOUR EYES AND SEE THEM.

#MOVETHECLASS

This focus on yourself allows room to be more comfortable, and that comfort opens opportunities for exploring new ideas and techniques to foster greater Achievement from students. Will there be mistakes along the way as we teach our students? Absolutely. As human beings, sometimes we disappoint ourselves; it's natural. Most times we are disappointed because in some way, we've fallen short of our own expectations As a result, we often punish ourselves through guilt, fear, or shame. Whether the situation is we don't feel like we're making enough of a difference, didn't stick with our diet or fitness plans, or wish we would have reacted differently with a student, co-worker, or family member, somehow we've messed up.

What's worse is that any time you're reminded or think of a time you made a mistake, that same guilt or shame resurface inside you. It is terrible that we do this to ourselves unnecessarily. To change this starts with Awareness, recognizing that we needlessly suffer over and over for debts we've already paid. Focus of self allows you to make those mistakes with an understanding that those mistakes provide growth and learning, critical factors for educators. That's another way to discover what works for you, by understanding what doesn't.

Remember, as we focus on becoming a Master of the Mix, we're trying to find that delicate balance in our classroom, one that is not too far to the left of the fader and out of control, nor too far to the right of the fader, where we have too much control. As a Master of the Mix, blending my self-care, health habits, and personality with the other elements of Achievement and Alliance was critical. When I began to understand the impact my life outside the classroom had on my life inside the classroom, it helped me fine-tune important aspects of my teaching.

End Notes

The Track title is a play on the lyrics from "99 Problems" (Jay-Z, 2004). Roc-A-Fella Records

TRACK 7

ARTISTRY - CREATIVELY, TODAY WAS A GOOD DAY

Creativity and innovation in the urban classroom

I define Artistry as the act of influencing something with imagination and creativity. You know something involves Artistry when the end result has many possible outcomes and is affected by your individuality or original ideas. Many times, this results in an experience for the end user or others, and provides a level of satisfaction to person who created it.

Let's use for an example adding two plus two. This is not example of Artistry because your creativity cannot influence the outcome. The answer will always be four, regardless of what you do. On the other hand, let's look at cooking. Something as simple as cooking a hamburger allows you to demonstrate Artistry. So much imagination can go into how it is prepared, what toppings are used, and how it is served. The ability to demonstrate all kinds of creativity with a sandwich and creating a palatable experience for whoever is lucky enough to consume it, that's Artistry. Or how about music? From the different genres and styles, melodic and rhythmic combinations, the options are literally endless and there is often a high level of satisfaction for both the creator of the tune and the listener. This is a prime example of Artistry because creativity and imagination are at play and influence the outcome.

You know what else allows you to demonstrate Artistry? You guessed it—teaching. Everything from your classroom decor to your lessons can be influenced by your imagination and creativity, crafting an experience for you and your students. That is Artistry at its finest.

One of the key components of Artistry is taking advantage of our ability to create. This is so powerful because I think this speaks to who we are as creational beings. Not to get overly spiritual, but if you think about it, God "created" the Heavens and the earth; root word being "create." So, if we are made in His image, doesn't that mean that, to some degree, we were placed on this earth to "create" as well? From that, I can draw the conclusion that if we are placed here to create—to demonstrate Artistry—then it is from creation and Artistry that we derive satisfaction and fulfillment. It is my belief that we as "creational" beings thrive while creating in its many forms. Something, regardless of what it was, that wasn't there or didn't exist, now exists because of you and your intrinsic desire to create. Even the act of re-creation offers that same sense of satisfaction because although you followed that recipe for that mouth-watering dish, or those instructions to build that chest of drawers from IKEA, you breathed life into what now exists, solely because you took the time to create.

 EVERYTHING FROM YOUR CLASSROOM DECOR TO YOUR LESSONS CAN BE INFLUENCED BY YOUR IMAGINATION AND CREATIVITY.

Ever since I can remember, I thought there was something almost magical about a good DJ, someone who generated so much energy, good vibrations, and fun with mere records. As I grew older, I came to have this same appreciation for good educators. Someone who can take a subject that may have the interest level of watching paint dry and turn it into a learning experience for their students is literally an Artist in those moments. Each and every time we step into the classroom or sit down to design learning experiences for our students, we demonstrate Artistry through creation. What I came to learn was that the magic lays in what that DJ and educator brings to those songs and subjects. All kinds of Artistry emerged from their individuality and passion. It wasn't just a crate of records, or it wasn't just science. It was an opportunity to create with songs and elements from the periodic table as the key ingredients. Because this was an experience for them, it became an experience for anyone who had the pleasure of being in the audience or classroom.

WHEN I BEGAN TO SEE MYSELF AS A CREATOR, A MASTER OF THE MIX IN MY CLASSROOM, I BEGAN TO FEEL MORE EMPOWERED.

Teaching is one of those careers that allows you to demonstrate Artistry in an almost unfathomable variety of ways. The more you do it, the better you get at it. When I began to see myself as a creator, a Master of the Mix in my classroom, I began to feel more empowered. With this power, I felt more in control of what I was able to do, of what I was able to get my students to do, and how I was able to do it. Bringing my individuality alongside with my content expertise to demonstrate Artistry in the classroom was extremely exciting. Moreover, it was evident to my students because they began to enjoy the lessons more. Artistry came out in the way I discussed the content, the way that I acted about the content, and the way the students received the content. It resonated for me and for them on so many levels, inviting them to develop the same love and appreciation for the content that I had.

WHAT CAN LIMIT YOUR ARTISTRY?

Innovation and creativity in the classroom that does not match the way your students understand the world leads to frustration. I know a great deal of educators, including myself, who made attempts to demonstrate their individuality and creativity in their lessons and learning experiences in the classroom. They take time to come up with different ways to convey an idea that may spark their students' interest with something a bit out of the norm. A lot of planning may go into place and even a lot of upfront excitement. You get to put a little bit of your personality into a lesson. You make all of this effort, and your lesson is still not well-received. You find that this, just like other lessons, has minimal, if any, impact and your Artistry is stifled.

We know as individuals we are creative by nature, and teaching is a field that allows us to bring our individuality and Artistry into the classroom, yet we find ourselves time and time again in situations where it simply does not work. It is hard to continue to demonstrate creativity when it's not well-received. Who would want to? Lessons that are not well-received often have us looking in the mirror with a feeling of failure and insecurity, so we revert back to what we did before, and yet often, returning to what was safe and comfortable still does not work.

If we take a look again at our discussion on culture, remember that from the student's perspective, there are norms and rules in place that everyone should understand and abide by. This includes how the student is taught. If instead, a teacher, although well-intentioned, runs the classroom in a way that does not align with the students' understanding of the world, their culture is diminished. At a fundamental level, it doesn't feel right to students, and many times, beyond just being uncomfortable, it can feel disrespectful or even offensive. This is because our personal cultures carry unspoken rules of what is considered courteous, acceptable social interaction, appropriate personal space, and so much more. Social violations of these types are deeply rooted into our emotions and offenses here are a one-way ticket to mistrust, stress, and social tension.

As educators, when we are in the classroom and we bring our individuality into a lesson or learning experience and mix it with a bit of creativity, it is so important that Artistry is built on the right foundation: the foundation of our students' cultural strengths and learning styles. We should capitalize on ways that they learn best.

Engagement is an outcome of **motivation,** which is an outcome of what we value, which is an outcome of our culture. Culture has a tremendous impact on how we learn, and when this is not considered, it's pretty much a guessing game as to whether or not a lesson will be successful. Traditional teaching practices that focus solely on memorization, individual worksheets and assignments limit student learning because they do not leverage intrinsic motivation. Teaching that does not give consideration to the culture of students in urban and culturally diverse schools promotes mediocrity.

When lesson creativity comes from the right place culturally and is well-received by your students, it provides the type of feedback and confirmation you need to keep creating. This results in better learning experiences that are even more creative the next time and continue to be well-received by your students. You begin to have these creative experiences on a regular basis, you enjoy the teaching more, and students enjoy their learning more. Another win-win.

FEED YOUR ARTISTRY

When I was first learning to become a DJ, I knew how important it was to be in the presence of a good DJ. I was fortunate enough to be able to learn from a DJ who became not only a musical mentor, but a good friend as well. My DJ mentor's name was Troy, but in venues all across town he was known as DJ Mista Nice—and he was just that, he was nice! Nice, as we called him, was the kind of mentor who was always certain to communicate with me honestly and let me know the thought process behind what he did and why. When it came to gigs and shows, he always communicated professionally with the promoters or vendors, showed up on time, and stayed until the job was done. In between the time when the event started and when it ended, the crowd always had a good time. Always.

In my humble beginnings as a DJ, Nice was kind enough to let me tag along with him any and everywhere he went. I took every opportunity to soak up and learn as much as I could. As a matter of fact, for that first summer I was practically his shadow. There would be instances where I would stand with him in the DJ booth and watch how he chose specific songs, when he chose to introduce them, and, when given the opportunity, ask why he chose to play things when he did. All of this allowed me to get into the mindset behind what it took for him to move the crowd. He was very, very good at what he did, and it showed.

Under his mentorship, I had opportunities to stand in for him during his time DJing. For example, he eventually trusted me to carry on the event for a few moments at a time if he needed to step away. In those moments, even if he was not in a place where I could actually see him or if I didn't notice him, he was always listening. Afterward we would debrief and I would ask him for honest feedback, and honesty is exactly what he gave me. He always told me, "I'm not going to sugarcoat it—I'm going to give the feedback you deserve and tell it like it is." At first, some of the feedback was difficult because I was trying my hardest but some of my transitions between songs or some of my selections didn't quite pan out the way I intended. But those were some of the growing pains that it took to become a good DJ and I did not let those honest moments stop me. I knew his feedback was what it would take to get better.

As time went on, studying from him and other great DJs, I got to a place where I was trusted to stand in for him for a whole show. So if there was a night when he was already booked or had an opportunity he was not able to take advantage of, he would call me because he trusted me enough to hold down that event and would vouch for me. I did not take those instances lightly. I always made sure that I brought my best to each and every one of those events. I was always professional and on time, and I made sure I moved the crowd. I was being trusted to represent someone else and did not want to squander that opportunity or future opportunities.

This type of mentorship was critical in the development of my specific and personal Artistry as a DJ because it allowed me to see many different instances of things that I could do, and test out these theories for regular improvement of my craft. From every observation experience, I learned. With every opportunity for feedback and discussion on what was done and how well it did or did not go, I learned. Not only did I learn, but it helped fuel my Artistry because I picked up techniques and style from Nice and made them my own.

This same type of learning also translates to the classroom. In my early days of teaching, I took many opportunities to observe other teachers for my own professional growth. From the requirements as a college student to have a certain number of observation hours, to my student teaching experiences as a participant in the action under some great educators, I took every possible opportunity to learn what I could. Even while an undergraduate student, I would sit in the classroom of great professors and not only take in the concepts of education and theory, but *how* those specific educators were teaching us, as the students, why they said some things, how students were reacting, and the results. All of these were opportunities for me to take their techniques and Artistry and adapt them to make them my own.

Mentorship was a huge part of my development as an educator. I'm so glad I recognized the importance of taking advantage of those opportunities. I learned by replicating many of the techniques and strategies I saw other educators use. I took the different strategies, methods, and teaching practices of others and adjusted them to make them my own. If there was an instance where I saw someone teach a specific concept I liked, I would be sure to take note either on paper or mentally of what the lesson was, how well it went, and how I could use it on my own. I can't even begin to tell you the number of times I did this.

And it was so useful to me. Sometimes, other teachers' methods worked for me, and there were some things that did not work for me. Regardless, I learned and strengthened my abilities as an educator.

The Beatles started as a cover band, taking the songs of those who inspired them such as Little Richard and Elvis. Kobe Bryant copied and practiced the moves of greats before him like Michael Jordan, the same way I tried to imitate what I saw from great DJs and teachers I was around. What you learn from these legends is that you can never perfectly replicate what the other person did. There's always something that's different. The Beatles' vocal timbre was different than that of Little Richard and Elvis. Kobe Bryant's body was not the same as Michael Jordan's, and for me, my teaching style was different because of my personality.

In each case, there are necessary adjustments that have to be made in order for imitation to work. It is in these adjustments where you begin to see how these specific techniques can work for you. You take what the greats do, adapt them to make it fit for you, and develop your individual Artistry. Just like that.

ADVANCED ARTISTRY—INNOVATION

Building on the ideas of Carol Dweck, Ph.D., in "The Innovator's Mindset," I like the way that George Couros describes the mindset of an innovator as *"the belief that the abilities, intelligence, and talents are developed so that they lead to the creation of new and better ideas."* A huge part of Artistry as an educator is taking our talents that have been developed through various means and using them as a source of innovation. As teachers of students of color, innovation is an important component of new and exciting ways to reach these learners. This focus on creation is where Artistry begins to flourish because it taps into and can influence our individual ways of thinking.

For example, it is impossible to deny the impact social media has had on our society as a whole. There are a great deal of ways you can demonstrate Artistry through innovation with social media. I'm a big fan of Twitter. I use it daily and find it so fun to interact and engage with others. One way that I like to do this is live-tweeting during special events and TV shows.

YOU TAKE WHAT THE GREATS DO, ADAPT THEM TO MAKE IT FIT FOR YOU, AND DEVELOP YOUR INDIVIDUAL ARTISTRY.

Live-tweeting during television shows is always fun because you get to see and experience your friends' and others' reactions to certain things in real time. It takes the experience of watching a show you already enjoy to the next level because it feels like you get to watch it among others. It enhances the experience and makes it more fun. It allows you to connect with others regardless of how far away they are, because in that moment you share the same experience of that show or event. It also allows you to get different interpretations, reactions, and feedback to whatever is happening, allowing you to get an inside look to others' perceptions of the same experience. This can be fun, engaging, and quite hilarious all at the same time.

When teaching your diverse learners, there is an opportunity to demonstrate innovative Artistry with Twitter. What would it look like to live-tweet with your students as a special assignment that you gave them to reinforce their learning? Live-tweeting a special program or event like a rare race shuttle launch or world event would be a good idea. Or how about a televised movie or program that relates to content being taught? The opportunities are endless here. Instead of tweeting about a Thursday night drama series, you're having just as much fun while interacting with your students and being involved in their learning. Do not forget that the idea here is to become a Master of the Mix, maintaining that delicate balance between chaos and constriction by balancing the four elements of urban education. Using Twitter in this example goes beyond Artistry because it crosses the bounds of Achievement and Alliance. It reinforces the relationships that can be fostered with students, while helping them learn in ways that are meaningful to them. See what I did there?

What you'll notice as you develop your Artistry is that you'll find more and more ways to be creative and innovative. You'll also find that this will rub off on your students in a positive way. You will be creating learning experiences for them, which will foster unique ways for them to demonstrate their knowledge and ability to solve problems. When your students are being taught in ways that help them learn, it encourages them to think in new and exciting ways that allow them to demonstrate their individuality as they solve problems both in the classroom and, later, in the real world.

When you demonstrate your abilities as a Master of the Mix, blending Achievement of your diverse learners with their culture in mind, along with using your Artistry to create

Alliances and Awareness, now we are talking about next-level teaching and learning unlike anything you have ever experienced before. A delicate blend of these four elements allows you to go beyond merely presenting content to creating continual learning experiences.

YOU WILL BE CREATING LEARNING EXPERIENCES FOR THEM, WHICH WILL FOSTER UNIQUE WAYS FOR THEM TO SOLVE PROBLEMS.

What will it look like in your classroom when you begin to teach in new and innovative ways that demonstrate Artistry? Have you begun to imagine yet what the possibilities can be in your classroom? Have you begun to see what can come about and how this can help you to thrive in your classroom? Have you started to get the taste of success for yourself as well as your diverse learners?

End Notes

The Track title is a play on the lyrics from "It Was A Good Day" (Ice Cube, 1992). Priority Records

SIDE B INTERLUDE

MISCOMMUNICATION LEADS TO CROWD COMPLICATION

*Knowing and appreciating your audience
so they'll respond in kind*

As a high school student, I got my first up close and personal experience with what it meant to move the crowd and was instantly drawn to the art of being a DJ and an MC. The year was 1999, my senior year, Long Island, New York. Our school didn't have a lot of parties for us, so when we did have them, the excitement was overwhelming. The particular party was positioned to be a great event, because anybody and everyone was going.

Tickets were sold, outfits were laid out, and fresh haircuts were on deck. Me and my friends arrived a good 30 to 45 minutes into the event because to be there early or even on time was lame. The party took place in the cafeteria, which was on the side of the building right off the main parking lot. So when we pulled up, all we had to do was hop out of the car and walk right on in.

We get inside the cafeteria to see the decor, the flashing lights, all signs of a good time. But as we exchange fist bumps and handshakes and take inventory of the scene, it becomes obvious that the dynamic of the party just wasn't there. It was dead. There was a large crowd and the music was blasting, but the energy was almost nonexistent. I stood by hopelessly and watched for the next 30 minutes as no matter what the DJ tried to do, no one budged.

Refusing to be a victim to the evening's boredom any longer, my friends and I immediately huddled up to devise a plan.

"We have got to do something! This is terrible."

"Where's Paul?" I asked.

Paul was one of my classmates whose hobby just happened to be DJing. Paul was a cool dude and we hung out a few times. I went to his house on a few occasions, where he introduced me to his turntables, two silver spectacles of pure elegance that rotated records with ease, gliding across the slipmats like ice. He showed me a few different times how to properly place the record on the platter, put the needles in the groove, and even scratch. I was in heaven. Right in his basement I'd seen him blend, mix, and move from song to song in a calculated, but effortless, fashion. I knew he was the guy for the job.

Knowing that Paul was a dope DJ, I made the bold decision to find him and let him know we had no choice but to get his equipment and relieve the gentlemen from his duties if we were to save the party. And that is exactly what we did. Thinking back on this now as an adult, that was terribly rude of me, but we did what needed to be done in that moment.

So with that, we left the party, drove about 10 minutes around the corner, loaded up Paul's turntables and records, and headed back to our school's cafeteria with a renewed sense of confidence that we were going to save the night. As we arrived, we signaled for some others to come out and help gather the equipment, because we had a lot. Each person grabbed a crate or turntable and we proceeded to head into the building. Getting everything inside, were so excited to get in there that I honestly do not remember if the car was ever turned off or not. In that moment, it didn't matter.

As we walked into the stagnant crowd, I recall trying to inform people we needed room to get through. I held one hand up to my ear and used the other to gesture that we needed people to move to either side, almost like a secret service agent clearing the way for a political dignitary. Moving through the audience, I saw faces light up in both excitement and relief. They saw that there was still hope for the night and in a matter of moments things could change.

Clearing a direct path to the front of the party, we kindly informed the gentleman that his services we no longer needed. In setting up Paul's equipment, you could *feel* the energy shift. He was beginning to move the crowd and hadn't played a single record yet. The turntables we plugged into the mixer, the crates of records were lined up behind him ready to go, and the mic was switched to the "on" position. Paul's called out "Mic check 1- 2, 1-2," dropped the first record, DMX's "Get At Me Dog,"[1] and that was it. The party went from zero to one hundred so fast it almost made your head spin. He followed that first song, one after the other, in a way that made you feel like you had no choice but to enjoy yourself at that party. Effortless transitions, high levels of energy, and expertise of content at its finest.

That particular moment solidified it for me. Watching magic happen right before my eyes, commanding and getting back the energy needed to move the crowd, felt downright exhilarating. But what this experience taught me was that although the first DJ had all of the right equipment, the right songs, he was even likely trying very hard, there was clearly *something* missing and a huge disconnect, as he was in no way able to move the crowd. I had to make sure when my time came to be the crowd motivator, I was not only prepared with the right equipment but the right information as well. I would have to know my audience like the back of my hand.

End Notes

1. "Get At Me Dog" (DMX, 1998). Def Jam Recordings

The Side B Interlude title reflects lyrics from "Lost Ones" (Lauryn Hill, 1998). Ruffhouse Records

TRACK 8

ALLOW ME TO INSTRUCTIONALLY REINTRODUCE MYSELF

Taking your teaching to the next level so that both you and your students soar!

Today, most of us will not use a new product or go to a new place until we check the reviews. Going to see a movie, we ask someone if they've seen it and whether or not they'd recommend it. We ask for recommendations for restaurants and what people liked about it and what their experiences were. When hiring someone for service such as a DJ, we want to know where they've been and how well they entertained their audience. What if we were to ask ourselves that same question about our teaching? Would my students recommend me?

Moving the Class begins with taking a good, honest self-inventory and asking some tough questions like this and others:

What do I really know about my students?

What's important to them?

What motivation am I providing for them to want to learn from me?

Am I connecting with all of my students?

Is my true creative self shining every day?

Am I allowing things I have no control over to impact my teaching?

To Move the Class, we're talking about teaching where "the how," "the what," and "the why" of learning are not only unified, but meaningful. Inner-city and multicultural students need to be taught in ways that accommodate the unique mix of race, ethnicity, class, and community, while contributing to their everyday cultural identity.

Your students, like Jonathan, the student from the introduction, are looking for connection. Connection to you and connection to the learning. When one or both of those things are not in place, it makes your job a lot harder and it makes disconnecting a lot easier for the children, which manifests in many, many different ways. The reason I was able to have such a strong connection to Jonathan for the year he was in my class and beyond was because that connection between him and the learning material was there. As a Master of the Mix, I knew when to dial up on my culturally responsive teaching so that the lessons matched my students' everyday lives. I also knew when it was time to dial back and turn up the levels on Alliance to nurture the relationship-building that was necessary to maintain my students' desire to want to be in my classroom.

YOUR STUDENTS ARE LOOKING FOR CONNECTION. CONNECTION TO YOU AND CONNECTION TO THE LEARNING.

When I began my teaching career, I did not have anyone break down to me how important these four elements of urban education were. You see, I got a late start my first year: I wasn't hired until six weeks into the school year. This was unusual because the position was not available just a couple of weeks prior. This particular school was a public school in the urban, southeastern part of Virginia, in a district that served over 30,000 students. The schools in this district varied significantly. Depending on the part of town, there were big differences in the buildings, resources, and student demographics. Because of where we were, we didn't have the new building, the 1:1 student-to-laptop ratio, or anything close to it. Before walking into that building on my first day, I did my research. When I told people where I was going to teach, responses echoed along the lines of, "Oh you're going to teach at *that* school…" or "I've heard about *those* kids…". Here's what I concluded from the data I gathered: the school was in an urban area, the neighborhood has its struggles, the students had run the previous teacher out of the building, and we were already six weeks into the school year, so I had no time to waste.

When I got into the classroom, I had to make up for lost time. This was a class where the teacher had quit after less than a month on the job. That right there told me the students I was to teach were going to be a challenge. I wanted to convey the message that I was about business and there we no games being played in my classroom. Zero. From the first day I walked into that building, I was buttoned up in a suit and tie, with shined shoes and a firm attitude toward this thing called teaching. I knew that I wanted respect, and I knew that at the age of 22 I had to demand it from day one. And that was what I did. My mission was to show them who's boss and make it very, very clear that I am *not* the one.

So when I walked into that classroom, having already decided what kind of students I was dealing with based on everything *but* my interactions with the students, I had cemented my paradigm and didn't even know it. Every day for my first two years of teaching, I wore a suit and a firm attitude. I did not smile much and often raised my voice. What I did not realize was the narrative I listened to about my students created a paradigm that would severely limit my success early in my career. My goal was not to Move the Class; my goal was to solely to control the class.

During my interview, the faculty members and administrators present talked about how wonderful the students were, how excited they were for their new teacher, and the great things they were doing. On the outside, I smiled in agreement and nodded with the anticipatory excitement. On the inside, honestly, I called BS, because I knew they had, not but a few days ago, ran their former teacher out of the building. I failed to realize that the faculty members were talking up the students for who they were, and I was drawing conclusions and creating this script about them based on who I *thought* they were.

My paradigm was flawed.

What I failed to realize is that I was taking on the role of a disciplinarian, to the point where I begin to invoke fear in my students. That, my friend, is not teaching. This came to head for me when I received a call from one of my students' parents that her daughter was scared in my class—not of other students, but of me. This particular student was not a troublesome student in any way, shape, or form, so when I received the call I was shocked. I wondered why the student had not said anything to me, but realized when I replayed some of the scenes from the classroom why this student was fearful of being there. I spoke with intimidation in my voice and leveraged that as a tool for classroom management. After all, I was teaching in an urban school and knew that discipline was the most important factor for learning in this type of environment, right?

I felt absolutely terrible, as this was not the type of teacher I wanted to be. This forced me to immediately make some changes. The next day, cautious in my approach, I sat down and had a heart-to-heart with this student to let her know that it was not my intention to be scary, and I apologized. I used that as an opportunity for her to see me as not just as a scary, dominant teacher, but as a human being and somebody who genuinely wanted the best for her but may not have gone about it the right way. I felt that she genuinely accepted my apology, and from that day forward it was the beginning of a new Mr. Woodly in that classroom.

After having this heart-to-heart, I realized she may not be the only student who felt this way; she was just the only student who I knew of because her parent told me. In the coming days and weeks, there was almost a 180-degree shift in the energy level of my classroom. There were more smiles, there were more hands raised, there were more "Hi, Mr. Woodly"s and "Have a good day, Mr. Woodly"s, and it felt great.

You see, early in my career I was the type of teacher that was too far to the right of the crossfader—I constricted the learning environment. But even after recognizing that, it was a process to find the right blend that worked for me and my classroom. I had to come to the understanding that there's a time and a place for every record to spin on my turntables. The wrong record at the wrong time can create an atmosphere you did not intend nor plan for, even with the best intentions.

What that also helped me realize was that just because my class was sometimes quiet didn't necessarily mean that they were learning. I mistook silence for understanding while teaching, when often it was fear. That fear impacted their willingness to raise their hand and participate, so when they didn't understand the topics I taught, they were in no way willing to raise their hand and ask for clarity or help. Realizing this and how many opportunities I may have missed to help my students engage with and learn the content was troublesome for me, but I took that as fuel to move forward and make sure that I created an environment where these students felt emotionally safe at all times going forward.

In my early days as an educator, I wish someone would have told me about the power of Alliance and my level of Awareness, and how building solid student relationships that transcend academics is about understanding both sides of the equation: myself as well as my students. I wish someone would have mentioned the important role of culture and how much of an impact it has on my students' Achievement. Perhaps I would not have been so quick to jump to conclusions as a new teacher. I wish I would have known that feeding my Artistry as an educator was dependent on the right foundation, and how much fun it is to watch and see the results of next-level creativity in action.

Whether you are like me, a semi-Joe Clark in the classroom with the crossfader too far to the right, or your situation has left you with the crossfader too far to the left and things get out of control, I am telling you, you can become a Master of the Mix and create that next-level, all-engaging classroom environment. By reading this book, you are well on your way.

Let me tell you something. I want you to understand this very clearly. You do not have to settle. You don't have to be one of those people who just gets by day to day. There are far too many educators who do not realize how much control they have over the success of their classrooms. You have the ability and the opportunity to change the outcome. Using the elements of urban education will allow you to be a Master of the Mix, balance the crossfader, and stay away from the edges of chaos and constriction for a learning environment that is like no other: a classroom culture that is contagious with enthusiasm, positivity, and genuine excitement for learning. This type of environment feels electric, it feels inviting, and, moreover, it just plain feels good.

 ## YOU HAVE THE ABILITY AND THE OPPORTUNITY TO CHANGE THE OUTCOME.

Facilitating an experience for a crowd, be it at the club or in the classroom, is nearly impossible if you're ill-equipped. You, as the source of stimulation in your classroom, can take your catalogue of learning objectives and create an exchange of energy to curate a classroom culture that breeds joy in learning. Becoming a Master of the Mix is all about becoming proficient in each of the elements individually, then combining them in ways that work best for you to take your teaching to new levels. Using the elements of urban education will transform you into a one-person powerhouse, with the ability to transform a collection of learning objectives and lessons into an engaging, next-level, cosmic experience for you *and* your students.

I'm willing to bet that, to some extent, you are mixing and blending in your classroom right now, but perhaps there are times when an imbalance takes you too close to the edge. Maybe you have a good Alliance with your students but there's room to strengthen your Awareness so that you don't veer too close to the bounds of constriction. Perhaps your Artistry levels are off the charts but your culturally responsive Achievement can use some fine-tuning to keep the crossfader away from that side of chaos.

We have aspirations to change the world one student at a time, but when we're faced with adversity, we get further and further away from these goals and lower the bar for our success. But when you internalize and use the elements of urban education, you position yourself to change the world by changing the outcome for those students. Moreover, you position yourself to raise the bar, no longer settling for anything less than maximum flourish.

WHEN YOU INTERNALIZE THE ELEMENTS OF URBAN EDUCATION, YOU POSITION YOURSELF TO RAISE THE BAR.

There is a lot of fear that comes along with teaching, especially when it comes to teaching in urban and culturally diverse schools. Different personalities, different backgrounds, and different learning experiences and learning abilities can raise a lot of questions about how to meet the needs of such a variety of people. You know that teaching learners with diverse backgrounds has been a challenge in education altogether. We have to be conscious about fear and its place in the classroom. When you are afraid, you cannot think clearly. Fear acts as a dam that blocks your personal abilities, talents, and fun as an educator. So when you walk into that classroom and teach from a place of fear because you feel unprepared or because you are not quite sure if what you're going to teach will resonate, you've already lost.

To attack this fear head-on, it is all about making small but intentional decisions that are heading in the right direction. As you see success with these decisions, they will snowball into other, better decisions and lessons taught that will reach and teach each of your students to help them achieve. Attacking fear head-on will build your confidence, which will build your craft as a teacher. When you see classrooms of teachers that Move the Class, you see an environment of excitement and engagement because there is absolutely no room for fear.

It is easy to become intimidated when it comes to things like instructional observations. When you're in the middle of a lesson and that administrator walks into your room, whether announced or unannounced, it can create a certain level of anxiety because you feel like you're being judged, and someone is looking for you to make a mistake. I truly believe that when administrators walk into our rooms, they want to see the best of us on display, but sometimes our mind plays tricks on us and we end up crumbling. This is especially true in situations where we know the levels are imbalanced and somehow the crossfader finds its way too far left, and our classroom is close to a state of chaos smack in the middle of when we're being observed. These are truly the worst of times right here.

But when you are Master of the Mix, you create a classroom environment and culture that is warm, inviting, and full of enthusiasm for learning. This can easily become a situation where you welcome the opportunity for someone to observe you. Imagine how good it can feel to know that the levels of Achievement, Alliance, Artistry, and Awareness are so well-balanced that you can't wait for someone to come in and observe you. It's possible because I've done it myself. Each and every day of instruction is your time to shine, your time to put you and your students' abilities in the eyes of administrators or any other faculty members who have the pleasure of walking into your room.

While becoming a Master of the Mix, in moments where you get stuck—that lesson didn't land the way you thought it would or you can't seem to break down the barriers to connect with that student—remember that using the elements of urban education is a continual learning process. You're going to continue to change, class after class and year after year. And that is a good thing! Without change, there is no growth. Expect the challenges, welcome the challenges, and know that any mistakes and mishaps along the way don't define you or your abilities to teach. You find me an educator who's never made a mistake teaching, and I'll find you a person who wasn't really teaching to begin with.

 ## EACH AND EVERY DAY OF INSTRUCTION IS YOUR TIME TO SHINE

So many get discouraged when things don't work out as they planned and, within a short period of time, they're ready to throw in the towel. We fully understand that we cannot plant a seed and expect to have a tree the next day, but sometimes forget that when it comes to our own learning and development. Growth as an educator is a continual process and you are not expected to become a Jedi master overnight. You can learn to reach and teach each and every one of your culturally diverse students, and have fun while doing it. Enjoy the process and savor each and every step forward you take toward becoming a Master of the Mix.

There are constant adjustments, constant revisions, and constant monitoring that is needed in this process, which is all in an effort to position you to be the best educator that you can be. There truly is a lot of excitement to be enjoyed on this journey, but consistency is the key for each of these elements. It is also important for you to understand that what it takes for you to be successful in each of these elements may not be the same as what it takes for someone else. We all approach life in different ways and we all approach teaching in different ways, too.

When you get to a place in your classroom where Achievement of your students matches how they interpret the world around them, and the Alliance that you build with them is a genuine connection, and your levels of Awareness and Artistry position you to shine in your own unique way, only then will you truly Move the Class.

And so I'll say again—*you can get with this*: Create a learning environment that helps culturally diverse students thrive, increasing your effectiveness and decreasing your stress, allowing you to truly flourish in the classroom.

Or *you can get with that*: Continue to just "get by," not enjoying what you do day to day, and not making a difference in the lives of those students who desperately need you.

The choice is yours[1].

End Notes

1. "The Choice is Yours" (Black Sheep, 1991). Mercury/PolyGram

The Track title is a play on lyrics from "Public Service Announcement" (Jay-Z, 2003). Roc-A-Fella Records

NOTES

Couros, G. (2015). *The innovators mindset: Empower learning, unleash talent, and lead a culture of creativity*. San Diego, CA: Dave Burgess Consulting.

Covey, S. R. (1998). *The 7 habits of highly effective people*. Provo, UT: Franklin Covey.

Dweck, C. S. (2008). *Mindset the new psychology of success*. New York: Ballantine.

Emdin, C. (2017). *For White Folks Who Teach in the Hood... and the Rest of yall Too: Reality Pedagogy and Urban Education*. Beacon Press.

Gay, G. (2000). *Culturally responsive teaching: Theory, research, and practice*. New York, NY: Teachers College Press.

Goleman, D. (1994). *Emotional intelligence*. New York: Bantam Books.

Hammond, Z., & Jackson, Y. (2015). *Culturally responsive teaching and the brain: Promoting authentic engagement and rigor among culturally and linguistically diverse students*. Thousand Oaks, CA: Corwin, a SAGE Company.

Jennings, K., & Petchauer, E. (2017). Teaching in the Mix: Turntablism, DJ Aesthetics and African American Literature. *Changing English, 24*(2), 216-228. doi:10.1080/1358684x.2017.1311035

Kafele, B. K. (2013). *Closing the attitude gap: How to fire up your students to strive for success*. Alexandria, VA, USA: ASCD.

Kleon, A. (2012). *Steal like an artist: 10 things nobody told you about being creative*. New York: Workman.

Lloyd, P., Fernyhough, C., Vygotsky, L. S., & Wygotski, L. (1999). *Lev Vygotsky. critical assessments: The zone of proximal development*. London: Routledge.

Pink, D. H. (2010). *Drive the surprising truth about what motivates us*. Edinburgh: Canongate.

Paradigm [Def. 3]. In *Merriam-Webster Online,* Retrieved November 5, 2017, from *https://www.merriam-webster.com/dictionary/paradigm*

Senge, P. M. (2012). *Schools that learn: A fifth discipline fieldbook for educators, parents, and everyone who cares about education*. New York: Crown Business.

Whitworth, L. (2009). *Co-active coaching: New skills for coaching people toward success in work and life*. Boston, MA: Davies-Black Pub.

Wlodkowski, R. J., & Ginsberg, M. B. (1995). A framework for culturally responsive teaching. *Educational Leadership, 53*(1), 17-21.

ACKNOWLEDGEMENTS

I am extremely grateful for the love and support of my wife and children. There is absolutely no way this could have been done without your love and support—and for that I say thank you! I would also like to acknowledge all of the great educators who have impacted my life in more ways that I can count. I would not be where I am today without your help, encouragement, motivation and most importantly love. Thank you.

Last but not least, I want to thank my wonderful parents and siblings. They each are the true definition of a "day one" and have supported and encouraged me in everything that I have ever done. Their support has always been unwavering and I am truly grateful.

JUST FOR YOU

Without a doubt, educators have the most important profession ever— this cannot be debated! Because we have such an important role, it is important that we be at the top of our game each and every day and I can show you how to do just that! Right now, for free, you can download my guide "10 Proven Methods for Top-of-Your-Game-Teaching as an Urban Educator" by logging onto:

www.ShaunWoodly.com/10provenmethods

Free?! Yes, free!

LEARNING ON THE GO

I wasn't always one to listen to podcasts, but since I started I am hooked! Podcasts are great because they allow you to learn and experience *so* much more even when you're on the move! That is why I have created *Teach Hustle Inspire*. In each episode, I share the best and latest research-based strategies of master educators to help you flourish in the classroom. These are classroom management, student engagement, teacher lifestyle hacks, and everything else that works (and doesn't work) to help you be the best teacher you can be! Check it out!

HAVE DR. SHAUN WOODLY COME TO YOUR SCHOOL OR NEXT EVENT

Dr. Shaun Woodly offers a number of exciting and engaging keynotes, professional development programs and educator workshops to fit your specific needs. These offerings help educators by giving them the strategies necessary to remove barriers that limit student success in the classroom. It affords teachers the opportunity to reach, motivate, and engage their students regardless of the challenges they face, setting the stage for the highest levels of student achievement!

WHAT ARE PEOPLE ARE SAYING ABOUT DR. WOODLY'S PROGRAMS?

"This was an extremely useful professional learning experience, Dr. Woodly!"

"Your presentation helped to motivate me and give me a better attitude and was fuel for me to be more creative with my teaching."

"Keep doing what you are doing, Dr. Woodly. The training was amazing! It was a confirmation to our mission and vision."

"I'm really glad that I came! I feel empowered to go in my classroom and make something happen!"

"There were a lot of things I can relate to. This is going to help us grow as a school because it was such great information. Kudos, Dr. Woodly!"

"It was very powerful to become more self-aware, and learn to help our children to be the jewels we know that they are!"

POPULAR MESSAGES AND WORKSHOPS
FROM DR. SHAUN WOODLY

Dr. Woodly's programs can be tailored to the needs of your school, district, or event. However, here are some of the programs and keynotes available:

MC Means Move the Class: The Elements of Urban Education Power Workshop

Classroom Management for the Urban Educator: Optimize for the Win-Win

Set It Up For Success: The First 6 Weeks of School

The Mindset of a Classroom Superstar

And more…!

LET'S CONNECT!

Contact Dr. Woodly for more details about bringing him to your school or upcoming event.

 ShaunWoodly.com

 shaun@shaunwoodly.com

 @ShaunWoodly

 facebook.com/teachhustleinspire

ABOUT THE AUTHOR

Shaun Woodly, Ph.D.

Lover of good BBQ, hip-hop, green smoothies and cool sneakers, I'm a Hampton University graduate twice over and studied at Capella University for my doctorate. At the end of the day I'm just a guy from New York trying to make a difference in the lives of our children—because they are our future.

#MoveTheClass

I would greatly appreciate your feedback on what chapters/tracks helped you most, and maybe even what you would like to see in future books.

It is my sincere hope that you enjoyed this book and found it helpful. If this is the case, please leave a REVIEW on Amazon so that other educators can find this and be informed as well!

Visit the website at www.ShaunWoodly.com where you can sign up for email updates.

Connect with me directly by email: shaun@shaunwoodly.com

Who's awesome? You are!

Thank you